CHRISTIANIT`
HAVE A FOl

Christianity, does it have a founder?

by
Felix van der Wissel

With a Foreword by Glen Reynolds

Translated from the Dutch original
by Anton van der Wissel
Amsterdam 2005

William Sessions Limited
York, England

ISBN 1 85072 331 1

Printed in 11 point Plantin Typeface
from Author's Disk
by Sessions of York
The Ebor Press
York, England

Contents

About the author

Felix Van der Wissel (1892-1962), stemming from a Mennonite family, has served as a minister in three Mennonite communities. He finished his studies and training as a minister in 1916, but refused to be confirmed in the office of minister, feeling ashamed over the tolerant attitude of the churches, the Mennonites included, towards the war and its atrocities. He became a schoolteacher, but after four years declared himself available as a minister for the Mennonite brotherhood.

He belonged to the few who stayed faithful to the Mennonite non-violent tradition. Being a minister he was exampled from military service.

His mini-thesis for his master's degree dealt with the original ideals of Saint Francis. Besides Saint Francis he was very much impressed by Gandhi and Tolstoy. Also by George Fox and the Quakers, belonging to the Wider Quaker Fellowship.

When invited to submit his candidature for the post of minister in the third community he served, a slander was spread about him being a communist. In that period just before-world war II, pacifists were as mistrusted as communists. So the association "Church and Peace" was forbidden to organise public gatherings!

During the German occupation he was engaged in finding hiding places for Jews and was confronted with the lack of civil courage in his environment. He was arrested by the Germans but had the luck not to be sent to a concentration camp, but to a work camp to help in constructing the Atlantic wall. He refused this work as a pacifist and risked being sent to a concentration camp; but was permitted by a friendly engineer–supervisor to be employed house keeping and cleaning of the camp.

He returned safely to the Netherlands. When he resumed his work as Minister, he was welcomed by the Mennonite community rising respectfully when he first entered the church.

A couple of weeks later he was invited to lead a service for the arrested "Quislings", Dutch citizens who had co-operated with the German occupier. He came home rather perturbed by the fact that this group too showed him respect and thankfulness for his ministry by rising when he left the church.

Felix Van der Wissel was one of the founders of the Mennonite Peace group and served this group many years as its president

In the forties and fifties he worked steadily on this manuscript as far as his duties as a minister allowed: a rather isolated scholar without an inspiring relationship with an university or a study group. The completed manuscript was found soon after his death in 1962 in a drawer of his desk. At that time it was submitted for publication. In spite of a positive scientific review the editor was not willing to risk publishing the work, because he feared the book at that time would not sell.

Now, over forty years, times have changed. Interest in this subject is far greater now than at that time. I am glad this essay is to appear at last, being still of interest and informative and a surprisingly early precursor to recent literature.

Anton van der Wissel

Anton van der Wissel, son of Felix, is a retired professor of psychology, state university of Groningen, The Netherlands. Though stemming from a Mennonite family he became a member of the Society of Friends (Quakers) in Amsterdam 1947.

Acknowledgements

I wish to express my gratitude towards all who helped to bring this book, in its English translation, to completion.

The original translation in my clumsy English has gone through several stages of rephrasing and polishing to arrive at the present form. The following friends, native speakers of English, took one or two chapters to deal with, Siobhan Wall and Andrea Parkes, attenders in the Amsterdam Quaker meeting, but also Quaker Friends from France, like Tony Hollingworth : a time consuming and refractory task to transfer the original Dutch text into clear English.

Marianne IJspeert helped me in completing the references of publications consulted.

Dennis Tomlin, who was fascinated by this manuscript, encouraged me to hold on - this essay was well worth publishing – and who, in the several years we worked together on the translated text, was able to identify with the author; for me a very special experience!

Nevertheless - pushed by his perfectionism - the often sermon like style was replaced by a more objective wording.

I accepted with great thankfulness the offers of Barbara Forbes and Suzanne Smith, two experts script-readers, to screen the manuscript for the quality of language.

I had the lucky chance to find Glen Reynolds - who is well at home in Gnosticism – prepared to write the foreword. So this essay - written in 1962 – now has a frame, which makes it clear that in fact it is still of current interest and takes its proper place among the books which have appeared about the origin of Christianity.

Lastly I wish to thank my publishers, whose patience and careful attention has brought my father's work to this final tangible result.

My gratitude towards all these, who helped me to bring into sharable form this "heritage", is as great as my satisfaction in having been able to bring to publication my father's work

Anton van der Wissel

Foreword

It is a great privilege to have been invited to contribute a foreword to this valuable study written by Felix van der Wissel some forty years ago. Felix would have been unaware of the contribution to an understanding of early Christianity that the subsequent publication of The Nag Hammadi Library[1] in the late 1970s was to have. Nevertheless his thesis arguments are a worthwhile contribution to the new interpretations born out by the gradual process of the publication of Gnostic texts throughout the second half of the twentieth century. Indeed, Felix refers to those early scholars of Gnostic understanding who have led to a belief that a meaningful interpretation and understanding of the New Testament Canon is not possible without consideration of those texts excluded from the Canon of the established Church, and now more recently of the Nag Hammadi Library

Felix identifies the significance of Alexandria in competition with Rome, as pivotal centres of academic thought that inspired the development of early Christian thought, not least in the concept of the Messiah and individual redemption. A key figure in the second century C.E. was the Christian-Gnostic Valentinus who was a contender for the position of Bishop of Rome and was deeply influential and based in Alexandria.

The substantial influence of Greek philosophy upon early Christian thought and on Gnosticism in particular, cannot be underestimated and Felix draws upon this weighty contribution throughout his work. Whilst the ongoing complex debate of the origins and definition of Gnosticism continues in Gnostic studies, the parasitic nature of Gnosticism and its syncretistic relationship with other faiths, including Hellenic thought and its impact upon the Old Testament and subsequent influence upon the New

Testament, is here identified by Felix prior to subsequent research which has corroborated this fact.

In particular, as a Quaker and a researcher into Christian (Valentinian) Gnosticism, I found the examination of the relationship of the divine spark/soul and the material world and human body, deeply illuminating. From the alienated individual seeking redemption from the material hostile cosmos and world, to the discovery of the divine within all human beings through a relationship with a redeemer figure such as Christ, Felix van der Wissel touches upon the psychological aspects of this process. In this he was a precursor to the interest of Carl Jung and his fascination for the Gnostic early Christians, including the subsequent ownership of what is known as the Jung Codex in the Nag Hammadi Library.

For many readers, especially Quakers, the concept of the immediate and individual redemption/resurrection, as opposed to any delayed eschatology of spiritual fulfilment, which Felix identifies in Alexandria thought, will be of significant interest. Moreover, as he correctly points out, the great scholar of Gnosticism, Hans Jonas (a student of Heidegger) identifies this in those early Christian Gnostics, as does the subsequent student of Jonas, Rudolph Bultmann[2] in his analysis of Gnostic influence upon the New Testament.

Also of interest will be the sociological aspect of the environment our of which an early Christian immediacy of redemption and heaven of earth now developed in Gnostic and Pauline thought. There is a pessimism which Jonas and Felix identifies in the social atmosphere – what scholars of Gnosticism view as social unrest arising from failed apocalyptic hopes and expectations. Life on earth was incompatible with the quest for the soul to become free of the material body in unity with God, Christ and the Heavens. The immediate, apocalyptic nature of the theology of George Fox (founder of Quakerism), at the time of the English Civil war, seminally identified by Douglas Gwyn,[3] replicates the development of Gnostic Christianity arising from failed eschatological expectations of a Messiah appearing in the flesh.

This book provides an extremely useful introduction to the studies published since the death of Felix van der Wissel. I commend it wholeheartedly.

Glen D. Reynolds

REFERENCES

1. *Nag Hammadi Library.* Facsimile Edition. 13 Volumes. Leiden: Brill, 1972-1978; *The Nag Hammadi Library in English* [NHLE] Revised edn. ET., members of the Coptic Gnostic Library Project of the Institute for Antiquity and Christianity, Claremont, California; Robinson, J.M., gen ed., Leiden: Brill and New York/San Francisco: Harper Row, 1978, 1988.
2. Gwyn, D. *Apocalypse of the Word: The Life and Message of George Fox (1624-1691).* Richmond: Friends United Press, 1984.
3. Bultmann, Rudolph. *Primitive Christianity in the Contemporary Setting.* Philadelphia: Fortress Press, 1956.

Glen Reynolds is a Quaker, Local Government Councillor in the UK, a lawyer and writer. His PhD *"Was George Fox a Gnostic"* was completed at The University of Sunderland, England, in 2004.

CHAPTER I

The Diaspora

Diaspora: definition and description

The word Diaspora means dispersion. It is usually applied to the dispersion of the Jewish people in ancient times and is still used in this way. But the phenomenon of dispersion is, of course, not necessarily restricted to Israel. There were other peoples who, in biblical times, endured similar events to those of the Jewish people, and had to undergo the same fate. That this does not seem obvious, is probably because those other populations did not remain united to the same degree as Jews; they mixed and were more assimilated with the peoples around them. Consequently, after some generations they no longer had a feeling of being 'dispersed'.

The Babylonian Diaspora

As for the Jewish people, who did have this sense of being dispersed, it is usually thought of in relation to the ancient Hellenic cultural area and later the Roman Empire. The Diaspora, however, was not only to the West (seen from Palestine) but also to the East. In 722 BCE and thereafter large numbers of people were deported by the Assyrian and Babylonic Kings to their territories in Mesopotamia. According to the inscriptions of King Sennacherib[1] not only the so called Northern Kingdom of Israel, but also a large part of the Southern Kingdom, Judea, was conquered. A total of 200,000 people were deported from 46 cities to regions in Mesopotamia. What became of this multitude in this foreign region is largely unknown, but it is difficult to believe that they exercised no influence at all on the surrounding inhabitants.

1

We only know from the book of Tobias, that there existed a large colony of Jews in the land of Medie; also that of those deported to Babylon, when set free by King Cyrus, the greater part stayed in their new country of their own free will, to which the books of Daniel and Esther also testify. This Babylonic Diaspora is important, because there was an intensive exchange after the exile between the Rabbis of Babylon and of Jerusalem. Thanks to the Babylonic Diaspora, the Jewish people did not perish after the demolishing of the temple. Hilleel, the well-known Rabbi, came from Babylon and the later very important Babylonian Talmud originated there. The influence of the Persians, who after taking Babylon, took control of Mesopotamia, was also important. It is quite possible that this change of regime was effected with the help of the large Jewish colony in Babylon and elsewhere in the East.

The Hellenic Diaspora

The Diaspora in the Hellenic cultural area is, however, more important for us in this study. Large Jewish colonies existed in Egypt, specially in Alexandria, on Cyprus, the Ionic Isles, Asia minor, Greece, Italy and North Africa (Cyrenaica). They came into existence as commercial colonies, by serving foreign states, by staying on of their own free will after deportation, by the liberation of prisoners of war and other causes. The communities they founded had, under the Romans, quite a lot of privileges, which could only be annulled by a decree of the Emperor. Such communities were allowed to found synagogues, prayer-houses and cemeteries and had freedom to use their own religious rituals; they were exempt from sacrificing before the statue of the Emperor (an exemption which was not granted to the later Christians). The communities could follow their own jurisprudence (except capital punishment) and had other similar privileges. It has been estimated that there were about four million Jews in the Roman Empire at that time, especially concentrated in the big cities such as Alexandria, Ephesus, Antiochus and Rome, among others. Naturally this massive number exerted a tremendous influence on the surrounding countries and peoples, even so strongly that Seneca in his time lamented: 'The teachings of these scandalous peoples have already in such a degree spread far and wide, that they have proselytes in

2

all countries; so the vanquished have imposed their laws on the victors'.

Some passages of R.M.L.Wilson, in his book 'The Gnostic Problem' (1958, p.3), serve to round off these facts and figures regarding the Diaspora:

'Alexander the Great and his successors thought the Jews to be excellent colonists for the newly founded cities in the Hellenic era whose rulers were for the greater part wholeheartedly willing to make use of the Jewish know-how in industrial and commercial fields. The Jews accepted cheerfully the advantages of this state of affairs.'

And M. Friedländer (1894, p.2) similarly: 'Alexander the Great after having been convinced of the solidity and reliability of the Jews, founded a Jewish colony in this city, to which the same rights and privileges were given as to his own Macedonian compatriots. After nearly three centuries this Jewish colony in and around Alexandria, by the industrious labour and an amazing activity on all fields of human life, had amounted to a million people.'

Friedländer also points out (ibid) that the successors of Alexander aimed at nothing so intently as making this city the centre of the whole culture of that time. The Museum and the Library of Alexandria, founded by Ptolemaeus Soter, lured whole swarms of scholars from all corners of the world to the city. Each scholar, independent of nationality or way of thought, found hospitality in the Museum, the costs being paid by the state. Not surprisingly, in this scholars republic many different nationalities and philosophical schools were represented and many different ideas flowed together or at least there was an exchange of reciprocally stimulating ideas. He then concludes, thinking of the spiritual development that resulted from all this: 'This melting of Greek and Jewish ideas within the city of Alexandria, caused indeed a great movement, out of which finally Christianity was born' (ibid p.4). We see there Friedländer's main theme and to a certain extent also that of the present author:- Christianity, developed gradually by Jews, was clarified by their contact with Greek civilization.

To get inside this process we must retrace its development in the Diaspora. The process is less simple than that described by Friedländer.

3

Diaspora: historic turning point in Jewish religion

The point in time when the Diaspora began seems to have been a turning point in the history of Jewish religion. From that time on the centre of gravity of Jewish religious life was no longer found only at Jerusalem and in the service of the temple, but also in the Diaspora, especially in Alexandria. A contrast developed between Judaism in Palestine, characterised by a tendency to close itself off from external influences and Judaism in the Diaspora, which was quite open to influences from the pagan world and in its turn had a strong influence on this pagan world. This phenomenon even went so far, that the words of Isaiah: *I made you to be a light for the pagans, that you might be of salvation to them until the ends of the earth* (Isaiah 42;6 and 49;6) have been attributed particularly to the dispersed Israelites and their proselytes (followers) among the pagans.

On the Jewish side it was even felt that the religion of Moses was the perfect world religion and a perfect legislation for the whole world, destined to become the foundation of world citizenship and to provide all people on earth with the highest happiness. Among the Jews it was hoped, not without reason, that at a given time men would put aside their own laws and religious observance and would prefer to live following only Jewish law and practice.

They even imagined that the highest purpose of Moses himself had been to establish everywhere concord, friendship and equality, which would bring for all humanity the highest bliss. To achieve this all peoples should forsake their idols and accept Jewish monotheism. But before arriving at that point a whole spiritual development had to take place, a process which we are accustomed to indicate with the word syncretism (merging, especially of religions) and which we will analyse in more detail in the following chapters.

Syncretism, exchange-market of spiritual values

Here we should point out the fact that each people, including the Jews, entered this domain of ideas with their own spiritual baggage, which they offered metaphorically speaking, to trade, in exchange for the values of other peoples.

The Jews entered this arena richly possessed of spiritual values: - a couple of instructive ancestral myths and legends, the figure of a God, who speaks to the guilty human: *Adam where art thou?*, a legislation of high moral standing. A number of prophetic figures evoking everyone's respect, speaking to the Kings of their age: *You are that man,* or *You did wrong in the eyes of the Lord.* They also addressed the people, preaching of justice as did Amos, of the conception of grace as did Hosea, of visions of the future as did Isaiah and Mica concerning a reign of peace, where men would melt swords into ploughshares, and pikes into sickles. In short, they came with a moral-religious life of high ethical standing.

Stylistic devices: parable and personification

In addition to the quality of this spiritual heritage, the form in which it was expressed is noteworthy. The parable is frequently used, for example by Nathan, facing David in the parable of the single ewe lamb, taken from the poor by the rich. Also used by Jonathan, confronting the claims of Abimelech, when he refers to the trees of the wood which want to choose a king and finally, while all other trees and plants refuse, arrive at the thorn bush. The parable is a stylistic device when one wishes for one reason or another to indicate the truth in a disguise. There is also personification, probably stimulated by the contact with the Persians, who considered all sort of ideas and virtues as more or less independent characters or personalities. This is very clear in Proverbs 8, where we find Wisdom portrayed facing Lady Foolishness. Lady Wisdom invites all travellers to enter her home to be refreshed with her wine and bread, understood as her spiritual gifts, which will make humans happy, in contrast with the ruination they experience following Lady Foolishness. Variations on this type of representation are frequent. A step further occurs when this personified Wisdom is incarnated in individuals and even in actual peoples. Jesus Sirach sees Wisdom especially revealed to Israel; in his opinion she is incarnate in this special people. The related idea is also found, namely, that Wisdom is identified with Jewish law. In the book Baruch (p.37 ff)[2] Wisdom appeared on earth and travelled among men. She is also identified as the book containing the commandments of God, the Law which exists in eternity. Again with Jesus Sirach (24:7-12) one finds: 'I (Wisdom) served in the name of God in the holy tent and to me was given a permanent dwelling in Zion. I took root in the praised people'. He is probably thinking of the meeting-tent in the desert, where Moses met with God and Joshua served Him, and the subsequent building of the Temple in Jerusalem. But, said this author, instead of the representation of God, it is God's wisdom that is dwelling in this Temple. To conclude we cite Solomon's book of Wisdom (7:26-28): 'She is a portrayal of God's goodness; from generation to generation she chooses her dwelling in holy souls'. Here the dwelling of Wisdom is already thought of as being wider than simply Israel, even if the incarnation in Israel formed the basis for this passage. Later on just such an enlarged incarnation idea will play a role in the spiritual development during the Diaspora.

We will not go into the oriental metaphorical language and symbols, because this is a well-known and widespread phenomenon, found also, of course, in Judaism.

But regarding all those stylistic phenomena, it should be emphasized that they already existed in Israel before the Diaspora. With these spiritual possessions, to use a strong image, the Jewish people is projected into the whirlpool of religious syncretism. We will try to demonstrate in more detail what grew out of this.

CHAPTER II

Syncretism

Syncretism: an outline

What would happen if so many different religions came into contact with each other? The first reaction would be to reflect on one's own religious heritage. Certainly, criticism of the unfamiliar 'other' would be quite natural. However in the light of that 'other' phenomenon, the positive aspects of which merit recognition, self-criticism would occur. This would result automatically in a deepening, which permits Quispel (1951, p. 21) to say, 'The deepening of the inner life and introspection is a characteristic of this time'. Thus might develop a sort of philosophy of religion, which could have as a consequence the attempt to reduce all religions to one primordial type, because in the foreign forms are found the same phenomena, but with different labels. Hence Isis, the goddess venerated in Egypt, says that, although she is the same goddess, she is adored in different ways and with different names by many peoples. 'The Phrygians call me'. she says, ' *Mother Goddess*; the people in Attica *Minerva* (Athena): the Cyprians *Venus*, the Cretans *Diana*, in Sicily I am called *Proserpina* (Persephone); in Eleusis *Ceres*; some call me *Juno*, others *Bellon*, but only the Egyptians call me by my proper name, *Isis*' (Reitzenstein, 1927, p. 240).

This self-criticism gets even stronger when one's own religious ideas are confronted with the philosophy of those days. Then one has to conclude repeatedly that one's own ideas, cherished from childhood on, are 'absurd', or have to be interpreted in a totally different way than that to which one is accustomed. The Greeks had already, before the time of syncretism, gone through this process, as far as it concerned their own religion. The Gods, whose singular adventures must be considered quite amoral, are interpreted as the personified forces of nature, their marriages or erotic relations as the conjunction of sky and earth. Rain and thunder also given meaning in this context. In the end there remains very little of the original meaning of these figures as found in Homer and other poets. It is important, however, to investigate in order to discover whether religion, in its original form, will still have some authority and also out of respect for these inspired poets, who cannot be accused of being absurd.

This process takes place with all religions involved in the process of religious blending. They all fade and become different from what they originally were, because a deeper and hidden meaning is given to the original words and images. Everything becomes metaphorical, the meaning of which has to be discovered and understood if one wants to reach the true meaning of the religion concerned. Hence out of the ancient religious forms, influenced by syncretism, new and original forms emerged, called 'mysteries' because they were offering insights which remained mysterious for those who were unable to recognize the deeper meaning behind the colourful representations. This very wide-spread development permitted Leisegang (1955, p.2) to say: 'Not one occidental religion escaped the fate of being changed by the influence of Greek philosophy into a form of profound mysterious wisdom'. Reitzenstein (1927, p.16) can say it with even more emphasis: 'The conceptions within religions become broader and deeper. This levelling and deepening tendency reached from Egypt to the borders of China'. Analyzing this process he says: 'Each religion has to change itself during the Diaspora, to become infinitely more individualistic than within a closed national society, where the meaning is quite clear, creating no problems for the individual; and on the other hand more universal, destined for all humanity and not only for one people' (Reitzenstein, 1927;p.17).

Influence of the Greek philosophy on Judaism

This overall development holds for Judaism in the Diaspora as for the other oriental religions, with the exception that Jews were more influenced by Greek philosophy than by Greek religion (or any other religion) because they thought of the respective Gods and rituals simply as idols and idolatry. At best they equated these Gods with Angels or Demons. But the influence of the philosophy, indeed of the whole culture of Hellenism, was considerable, so great that it was considered a matter of honour to master the Greek language as elegantly as the Greeks themselves. Indeed, tragedies were written in the Greek language, but in that case mostly with a Jewish tendency, for instance an Alexandrian Jew dared to rewrite the story of the poet-singer Orpheus, but having him sing the praise of the Jewish religion! One book is known, written from a Jewish perspective, with an oracle by the Erythrean Sibyl. She is a figure belonging to the Roman pantheon, but in this version the fortune-telling priestess makes all sorts of prophesies unfavourable to the Romans, putting forward the ideal of a kind of religious communism like that of the Essenes.

Here it is Judaism that opens the attack, addressing itself openly to the pagans. The main points of this preaching were especially: - monotheism – abandon the worship of the idols – and conversion from a too corrupt way of life to a way of life pleasing to God.

Influence of the Septuagint on the pagans

The most important influence originated from the Greek translation of the Old Testament, the Septuagint, which considerably impressed the non-Jewish world.

What of the self-criticism, the fading of Judaism, as noted with other religions? What were the philosophical concepts which gave reason to take offence at much of what was handed down by the holy books of the Jews?

The dominating, general philosophy

After the schools of Plato, Aristotle, the Cynics, the Epicureans and the Stoics, gradually, out of elements of all these a sort of general philosophy had grown. Thus Posidonius[3] had developed his system, the main characteristics of which were as follows:- in the first place in this system there is a mystic tuning. The human soul is nothing but a spark of the divine - one has to follow the spirit which dwells in us to carry the divine spark in a pure way through this life. This reflects the dominant mood of those days. More pronounced is God's transcendence and the teaching of the Logos (the word of God), who connects the unattainable deity with the world. Because these traits can be found exactly reflected in the Jewish literature of that time we describe this more extensively following Wilson (1958).

The Platonic view, quite generally held, was of a sharp separation between the ideal world and the world as our senses can perceive it. This ideal world – or world of ideas - was to be found above the seven transparent spheres in the sky (heaven), to which the planets were fastened. There, in the seventh (or perhaps eighth heaven) dwells the transcendent God, which meant God as a being beyond comprehension and in no way observable. Next, was a cherished idea that the human soul is a spark of the divine fire enclosed in matter, something divine imprisoned in a foreign, hostile element. The soul has to be freed so that it can return to the elevated world where it is at home. There are different ways to achieve this and the result then is that the soul attains immortality, or even becomes similar to God. Strictly speaking, this God is too sacred to have even the slightest contact with the material world, the world of matter, in which the soul by the Fall, or some other tragic event, is imprisoned. Hence God has to act upon this matter by means of his forces, which are considered as independent beings, the head of which is the Logos, the Idea of Ideas, which functions as a sort of mediator between God and the world. This Logos, or divine reason, is present implicitly in everything created, but has, in the human being, to develop conscious self-knowledge and knowledge of God.

Here there is a strong dualism: God is: 'He who is', of whom nothing can be said, opposite to the observable, phenomenal world, which has particular qualities which we can observe - God is spirit, and spirit is sharply opposed to matter. This, however, is a dualism destined to become a monism by means of the soul that has to be liberated out of its alien environment and becomes one with its primordial source or essence.

Influence on Jewish devotion

These and similar thoughts affect Jewish devotion. It is evident that much of the material of the Old Testament is not acceptable, seen in this light. It is clear that all anthropomorphic representations of God – His walking in paradise, His repentance over the deluge, His not-knowing about many circumstances about which people have to tell him – all such must fall out of use. The proscriptions of the Law and its difference between clean and unclean animals, its strange sacrificial rituals and meticulous rules concerning the priesthood – how are these reconcilable with the reasonable wisdom demonstrated by philosophy? What could those people who were exposed to the contemporary culture do with the popular stories and outspoken nationalist expectations? What to do with a Messianic figure who was presented as a hero, who will conquer the pagans and bring the chosen people to glory? In this clash of opinions, surely many people lost their faith, as is the case in the book Ecclesiastes, where faith can no longer be found and whose only enunciation is: *Vanity of vanities, all is vanity* (Eccl. 1:2) therefore suggesting a total aimlessness. There were Jews, at that time, who rejected Judaism as idolatry and became 'Greek' – without asking whether the Greeks of that time had not also arrived at the end of their wisdom!

So, one result of syncretism could be to lose one's faith. The majority preferred another way. This was to hang on the authority of the old books, but in such a way that these were given a deeper sense, as happened with other peoples. The Jewish religion thus became one of the many mystery religions, like so many already in the world of the Diaspora.

This statement could easily be contradicted, because it is customary to depict the Jews of the last centuries before Christ as exclusive, averse from interference by other religions. This latter is true, however – with reservations – only for Palestinian Jewry. The situation with Diaspora Jews was quite different. An author who devoted much attention to this contrast is the M. Friedländer already quoted who, by 1900, had already written several works on this subject but has since been ignored by theologians, both, Jewish and Christian.

Judaism and Greek Philosophy

Philo Judaeus, an Alexandrian Jewish philosopher, is one who shows concretely how the above mentioned difficulties were dealt

11

with. To remain in accord with the Greek idea of transcendence, Philo prefers not to call God by the name JHWH (this name being too sacred, was not mentioned by the Jews themselves). He uses instead 'He who is', or 'the Being', as in the Greek translation of the Old Testament in Exodus 3:4:. Here the overly anthropomorphic God of the Old Testament becomes the more impersonal Absolute of philosophy. The same is the case in the use instead of JHWH of the word 'God' or sometimes 'Lord'.

The Logos

The anthropomorphic behaviour of God is avoided by Philo saying (or the Septuagint translation suggesting) that it is not God himself, but an angel who acts, as is clear in the story of Jacob wrestling with a divine creature in Peniel (Gen. 32:22-32). Philo also often makes the Logos do and say what originally was attributed to God.

For him it is the Logos who leads the Jews through the desert as a pillar of fire; it is this same Logos or Wisdom, which takes the form of a rock that Moses beats upon to get water.

A symbolic explanation of the Old Testament

But here we see at the same time a symbolic reasoning appear, because Philo refers not to a thirst-quenching with ordinary water, but - what the divine Logos always does: - a quenching with God's spirit In the same way the manna is God's word, feeding the soul. The exodus out of Egypt is only a metaphorical representation of the liberation of the human soul out of the prison of matter. This is at the same time an example of how the national is replaced by the individual perspective. The strange proscriptions of the law about pure and impure animals are to be understood in a way quite different from that which the literal text implies: distinctions between good and bad people, virtues and vices, and suchlike.

Image of the Messiah as the ideal, wise man

Also the Messiah who will come, should not be represented in the popular way as a king, who will conquer the whole world for Israel, but as the ideal, wise man, who conquers the souls of men by his spiritual power.

Conclusion

In this way, in fact, all is transformed into reasonably acceptable values and in such a way that the Old Testament becomes acceptable for intellectual Jews as well as for cultural Greeks. The Septuagint is disseminated among the pagans and countless of them, who had rejected their ancestral beliefs, went over to this Jewish religion. This imposed on them no other obligations than those mentioned above, namely: - faith in the one true God and a pure, moral way of life. Even circumcision was no longer necessary for those new adherents of the Jewish faith.

This method of making spiritual all that gave offence, to give all things if necessary another meaning is called allegorizing, that is, systematic use of allegory (literally, saying another thing).

This phenomenon of allegory pervaded the remodelling process of Judaism so intensively that we will examine it in more detail in the next chapter.

CHAPTER III

Allegory in the service of Idealisation

Introduction

We have seen that the allegorical explanation turns up especially where one wishes to make the traditional authoritative writings acceptable for a modern world-view and conception of life. Allegory as a stylistic form is, however, much older. This is most evident in the case of dreams - a series of images which, superficially observed, have no sense (but nowadays are considered to be expressions of the unconscious). In antiquity a sense was attributed to these dream-images by considering them, for instance, as predictions of future events.

In the stories concerning Joseph this is very evident. Many prophets had visions, be it night- or daytime visions. But however important this stylistic form may be in general, what is most important here is the allegorical explanation of the scriptures of the Old Testament.

It was believed that the Holy Spirit always spoke in allegories or parables, whether figurative or metaphorical, but whatever one might call them they were always veiled - one had to discern the true sense. This arose because the existing text was nearly always allegorically explained. This is, for example, the reason that the Song of Solomon - in fact a collection of love songs – was included in the book of holy scripture. The description of a love-relationship was seen as a metaphorical expression of the relation between

14

God and the soul of the faithful. This belief in the poetic form in which God expresses himself, became so deeply rooted that even when they wished to produce a religious text, they reverted to this style. In fact the whole book of Hosiah can be explained in this way: the marriage bond of the prophet with his wife, an image of the bond between God and Israel. Ezekiel recounts several visions, which are ingeniously composed to veil and reveal hidden truths at the same time. Later this style is re-encountered in apocryphal books of the New Testament, such as "The shepherd from Hermas", and "The Barnabas Letter".

A tentative hypothesis: The Gospels as metaphor?

This gives rise to the question: - should not the whole collection of items, the New Testament of the Gospels, Acts, Epistles, etc. be seen as belonging to this sort of literature? It might then be seen, not only that Paul here and there used allegorical explanations of the Old Testament, but also that the whole story of the Gospels - even the 'facts', to put it bluntly, becomes one continuous series of metaphors and so becomes wholly an immense allegory. In this view, not only the healings by Jesus and others, not only the miracles would have a symbolic sense, but the thread of the whole story. This is a preliminary, tentative, hypothesis, but in the course of the present study there may emerge more supporting evidence for this hypothesis.

The allegorical method: risks

It was generally felt to be quite difficult to understand these scriptures. Of course the adherents of this method realized this too. They supposed that they needed a special higher knowledge to recover the hidden sense of the entire scriptures, a capacity that one could not acquire in the same way as scientific knowledge, but an understanding which was given by God himself to chosen humans. This higher form of insight is called gnosis. Now this method was acceptable only on condition that it be used by serious people like Philo. Philo in his written expositions uses play upon words, similarities of words which may be exchanged, numbers and their symbolic meanings and combines the Greek and Hebrew languages. What, however, would happen if less gifted persons used this method of writing and interpretation? This could easily result in degeneration of the text. For this reason, conservative Jews in Palestine, and later the Christian church when this institution began to constitute itself, always resisted this method. Therefore, for them, there could be no question of the idea that the New Testament also might be a spiritual creation of this nature. Nevertheless, it is a fact that at that time they wrote in this way and gnosticism (the system based on the use of gnosis), even though it often took a wrong track, also produced valuable things, so it is necessary to keep an open mind on this. This method of interpreting Holy Scripture was common among Hellenistic Jews in the Diaspora in those centuries, producing both a negative and a positive result. Negative, in so far as the Jewish leaders and authors explained away all sorts of material, which thereby lost its original meaning, positive in so far as they assimilated material, coming from the liberal circles of Greek culture.

The rejection of much material happened by keeping only those parts of the scriptures which were in line with what was preached to the outsiders: the adoration of one god (monotheism) and a moral way of life. Some went even so far that once engaged in 'interpreting', whole portions of the ancient scriptures were rejected. This was more specifically the case with the Law and it's multiple proscriptions and prohibitions. An antinomic party developed which rejected the law, a movement at one time so strong that it not only carried along the Jews of the Diaspora but even caused difficulties for the conservative Rabbis in Palestine. The books of Friedländer are very insightful on this subject. He defends the thesis that for a long period the Jewish Diaspora was sharply divided into two parties. There was a party faithful to the Law, in close contact with the conservative rabbis in the homeland, and another, which preached an unlimited universalism, which therefore by philosophical reasoning removed all meaning from the Law. Philo, who engaged a great deal in allegorical interpretations, kept nevertheless to the literal meaning of the scriptures and condemned the above-mentioned radical party. Those 'sons of the spirit', who vaporise the ritual law, should, in his opinion, be banished - sent out of the community. It was accepted that once the Messiah arrives, the law will be abolished, but as long as this event is only anticipated, one must still be faithful to the Law, even when looking for its secret meaning. Here can be found, long before Paul, the point of view he took regarding the law. With the difference that, for Paul the coming of Christ lay in the past, but for the Jews in these earlier centuries we are speaking of, the coming of the Messiah lay in the future. Friedländer says that the message of a religion emancipated from the Law, was already preached in the pre-Christian Diaspora. Accordingly, in his opinion, Christianity was in fact already born. He seems to detect a covert agreement between modern Christian and Jewish theologians to maintain the same misunderstanding about the origins of Christianity. The motive is, as already mentioned above, that they do not like to be reminded of the relationship to the Gnostics, while in his opinion Christianity developed naturally from the Jewish 'gnosis', as described.

This theory, will be tested, as far as is possible, against known facts, but first it should be noted that what Friedländer called 'Christianity' is rather negative, it was only the abolishment of the Law. Here we are looking for more positive values which belong authentically to Christianity but which probably originated among the Diaspora Jews. What positive aspects are offered by the Jews of the Diaspora who had, more or less radically, rejected the ritual Law and placed full emphasis on man's moral way of life?

The primordiality of a pure, moral life

The pre-Christian philosophers

Concerning this last aspect, a similar primordiality of practice can be found in the philosophy of the centuries before Christ. The study of physics had been given up as a fruitless occupation.

Epictetus (see Bonhöffer, 1911) said it quite distinctly: 'Does it concern me whether all things consist of atoms or of fire, or of earth? Isn't it sufficient to know the essence of good and evil?' He expresses the same thought, which was more or less the general mood, more systematically as follows: The first and most necessary part in philosophy is the part that deals with applying rules, for example; not to lie. The second part deals with proving, for example, why one should not lie. The third part gives the axioms and the underpinning for these proofs, for example; why this is a proof, what does it mean to be 'proving something'. This third part is partly needed on account of the second and the second on account of the first; The most urgent concern is the first.

What exactly is this praxis?

Seneca, the famous Stoic philosopher, speaks of charity: *Caritas generis humani*. Concerning the Stoics, his own philosophical school, he said (in: *De Clementia;* see *Opera*):'No school of thought is more kind and mild, no sect more philanthropic'. It is remarkable that he makes a claim identical to that made by Philo for Mosaic law! The Cynic – a related sect - puts himself totally in the service of God and therefore wants to live unencumbered, which meant unmarried. He calls himself a follower of Hercules, who had to perform twelve humanly impossible and onerous tasks, so he was a volunteer in the battle against the desire for enjoyment and a zealous advocate for the purification of life. The moral corruption at this time was so strong, that a powerful response was needed. 'Aux grands maux les grands remèdes!'.

Nevertheless, Epictetus (see Bonhöffer 1911) sees this in his own way: 'Did you succeed in training your body in sobriety? Then don't show off. Do you want to train yourself in bearing privations? Do it for your own sake and not for those around you'. Are we reminded now and then by these teachings of Christianity? It is indeed remarkable to read from the Cynic Antisthenes that when Diogenes asked him for a skirt, he gave him the coat too. The similarity goes further. From Seneca comes the statement: 'May you be inspired in your acts by God. He lets the sun shine also for criminals"(*De Ben.* IV, 25, 1vv; in: *Opera*). Another maxim from the Stoics is: 'The empirical man is sick; he needs a doctor'. Again, from Seneca: 'Forgive them; all are unwise'. Epictetus' ethical model goes even further in its agreement with Christianity: 'Do you wish to be crucified, just wait, and the cross will come'(Epictetus: *Diatr. II*, 2,20). Seneca also said it like this: 'Noble men are sacrified, and this with their own consent'. Indeed, Plato (*Crito*, p.49) had already said: 'It is unbecoming to retaliate for injury with injury, whatever they made you suffer'. When Seneca {*De Ira* 2:32.2: in *Opera*) says: 'We will give anger the space it needs (not to resist it); vengeance, even if it seems righteous, is something inhuman', is similar to Romans 12:17 – 'Never pay back evil by evil'. Epictetus, when asked how he would take revenge on his enemy, answers: 'By being as good as possible'. Furthermore, he continues: 'The cynic lets himself be beaten like an ass and loves those who beat him'. Finally, Seneca says: 'It is an obligation to give help, even to one's enemies' (*De Otio*, 28:4 in: *Opera*).

This was the spirit or spiritual mentality of the purest and greatest among the pagans of those days. Of course they were exceptional but the same is true for those who really lived as Christians and also for the enlightened Jews, on whose ideas we are focusing here.

The pre-Christian Jewish literature

On consulting the pre-Christian Jewish literature, we find there the responses to these voices, or rather one should say they are joining together in the same chorus with voices mentioned above.

In the Psalms of Solomon[4] can be found, among other statements, the following: 'The sacrifice of the Lord is justice and pureness of heart and lips' (20:4) and 'The Lord did circumcise me by his Holy Ghost' (11:2). Here can be seen clearly a displacement of the centre of gravity, from ritual prescriptions to purity in the practice of daily life. A. Drews (1924, p.158) says of this: 'The author of the Psalms stands in the transitional stage from Judaism to Christianity'. It is evident that in this respect also Christianity continues the line of Judaism.

Next we refer to some passages of the work of Philo, De Humanitate. He states there that the teaching of Moses prescribes a pure humanity. To give some examples: There is the injunction not to mow all the corn of the field, but to leave some in the corners. This is a very old custom based on a particular tradition that considers it as a measure in the interest of the poor, who are permitted to harvest what remains and also to glean the ears fallen out of the sheaves. An animal, belonging to a friend or an acquaintance, when lost, has to be given back to the owner. But the same applies even if it concerns the cattle of one's enemy. One may not claim usury from one's brother. But who is the true brother in the sense meant here? Moses does not mean blood brother but all citizens or co-nationals. One has to lend cooperatively and to ask back nothing more than was lent, for the difference between interest and usury was not made at that time. In each seventh year the ground has to stay fallow, but the poor can keep what is still growing there. Indeed, in each 49th year any one who has lost land by misfortune will get it back. It is difficult to imagine the execution of such a measure and perhaps it seldom happened in practice, but here our only purpose is to describe the ideals of the Diaspora Jews and the reality is therefore irrelevant. Foreigners (strangers), so it was said, have to be received in the midst of the community like friends and relatives and should receive a fair share of all material and spiritual benefits.

'Surely', Philo said, 'so thoroughly human is the Law that it even describes the obligations we have to animals and plants!' It can be added that Philo forbade swearing. This is because this makes others suspicious that one is untruthful (see Friedländer: Apologetik, pp. 231-250).

These are clear rules for daily life, of which several are within our capability. When it comes to ideals - or rules - so demanding that they are barely practicable, then Philo refers to the Essenes, the dispersed communities, found everywhere, who lived separately from the surrounding population but had their centre by the Dead Sea. From the scrolls found at Qumran we have become better informed about the lives and thought of the Essenes. Here however we are considering not the reality of their thought, but what a man like Philo saw in them. For him, these Essenes are the epitome of fidelity to the Law of Moses, as far as Philo and his like-minded friends understood it.

The Essenes

Moses had forbidden people to accumulate treasure or fortunes but, on the contrary, gave the command to possess all earthly goods in common. The Essenes were characterized most particularly by the fact that they did indeed live in agreement with this, as was evident from the literature found from that time. This continues our interest in the thought of Philo when he says that they had overseers for property held in common, who also had to look after the necessities of life from the joint revenues of the community. The division of labour and control of common property were placed under the responsibility of the administrators. Only one exception is explicitly made: each individual is free to help other persons and to exercise charity. The wage they received for their work, was given to the administrators. Some people cultivated the land, others became artists or artisans, but only when it served to enhance peace and benefit the general community (as understood in the broadest sense). They show charity to their fellow man, who ever he may be, by being benevolent. Their highest aim is to question whether their behaviour is in agreement with the love of God, love of virtue and love of their fellow man. This will be enough for the Essenes, who for Philo are the servants of God, the true disciples of Moses, in whom the depths of his teaching were inculcated. In Philo's opinion it was Moses who founded the true religion as a mystery, in the spirit of the other mystery-sects and only those who attained a higher knowledge and understood his deeper purposes, can be considered as his true followers.

One last point however has still to be put forward, mentioned this time not by Philo but by his near contemporary, Flavius Josephus, in his book "The Jewish War" (*Bellum Judaicum*, II, 8, 10). This deals with the events about 70 CE, when Jerusalem was conquered by the Romans and subsequently destroyed. Josephus mentions here the extraordinary courage of the martyred Essenes. 'They despised' so he writes, 'their pain and were upheld by spiritual energy. They considered an honest death better than a long life. In the war against the Romans they showed the strength of their conviction. Their enemies tortured them with screws and stretched out their bodies on the rack, tore their limbs out of their joints or burnt them. In spite of the most cruel application of these instruments of torture, nobody was able to extort from them a single depreciative word concerning Moses, their legislator, or even managed to entice them to take a forbidden food or to shed tears. On the contrary, they smiled during their pain and mocked those who adjusted the instruments of torture. They ended their life joyful as something that would be given back to them'(see also: Van der Woude, 1957 p.197).

One may ask why the Romans had such a grudge against these kind humans. The answer is probably that the Essenes saw the Romans as the enemy of the end of time, the instrument of all Evil, against whom resistance was an obligation and against whom one had to fight without mercy. In the eyes of the Romans they were clearly subversive fanatics who deserved no mercy. Such an extreme attitude on eschatological grounds is quite frequently observed. This example depicts the ideals cherished in the circles of the liberal Jews, even, if necessary at the cost of being martyred.

It is evident that the conception of God agreed with those practical ideas. Philo says, speaking of the general moral corruption: 'The human being, realizing his insignificance and sinfulness will bow humbly before God, who in his mercy, comes to the person, when he or she 'opens' him or herself'.

This 'opening of oneself' is essential. It is that which people can, for their part, do. God forgives and is patient. He is the saviour and is merciful; nobody can earn mercy or automatically deserve mercy. Indeed, Philo speaks many times of God's goodness and of God's charity, more often than of his judgment.

This shows how far the interpretation of the Old Testament by allegorizing has to go, if one wishes to reinterpret the God of Justice. This is the God who ordains the ban of the vanquished, which means the complete death of all men, women and children and also the devastation of the land. It is a long stretch to reinterpret this God as the God of love and peace, whom Philo preaches. It can also be seen here how this allegorising always follows a specific pattern. It doesn't proceed arbitrarily, changing without meaning the given into something different. Unconsciously - or sometimes consciously - the exegesis follows the cherished ideals. Those ideals are consistently those of love for mankind and fraternity, of peace and love for one's enemy, even to the acceptance of martyrdom. These ideals can be found not only among the Jews, but also in the works of the great pagan philosophers.

The next chapter will examine how this psychological pattern influenced the image of the Messiah as it took shape in the course of time.

CHAPTER IV

The material and its modellers

The Messiah in the Old Testament

The Messiah idea came into existence not as an image from the past but as one that would be fulfilled only in the future. There were a whole series of texts which could function as the building blocks for this messianic image, predictions concerning the coming holy era and the priestly prince who would then lead the chosen people. For example, in Isaiah the well-known words: *For unto us a child is born* are found (Isa. 9:6), taken as referring to Christ in many Christmas carols. In Isaiah it was a prediction for the future. It is noteworthy that the verse which uses the term 'Galilee of the Nations' (Isa. 9:1) has been interpreted as referring to the region where the Messiah, the child that has been born, will live.[5]

In such passages (when read with the necessary 'gnosis', that is, with the indispensable feeling for allegories) can be found not only a prediction of the countryside where the life of Christ will for the greater part be enacted, but also (again with the necessary subtle insight) the announcement that this preaching will for the greater part take place in the lands of the pagans. The same will be the case with Matthew 28:10, where Jesus says to his disciples: *Go and take word to my brothers that they are to leave for Galilee. They will see me there* (after his resurrection).

Isaiah (11:1-11) speaks of *he on whom the spirit of the Lord will rest* - and he who will found the reign of peace, where - *the cow and the bear will be friends* -. The Messiah will be a prince of peace, as

23

is predicted in Zechariah (Zech.9:9), *humble and mounted on a donkey.* Here the horse, associated with warriors, is explicitly excluded.

Micah (Mic. 5:1-4) teaches that the Messiah will come from Bethlehem. His name will be, according to Isaiah (7:14) 'Immanuel' (God be with us). Other names for him are: 'Son of God' (Ps. 2:7) and 'Son of men' (Dan. 7:13).

In Isaiah (52:13 and 53) the Messiah is described as the suffering servant of the Lord. He will act, according to Zechariah (4:6) not by force or by violence but by God's spirit. *He will,* again according to Isaiah: (42:1-7) *not break* a *crushed reed or snuff out a smouldering wick.* That is to say, He will uphold the weak and heal the sick. He will even be pierced, says Zechariah (12:10), so great is his meekness and passion. In Psalm 2: 8-9 others found a quite different prediction, namely, that the son of God would receive nations as his inheritance. This means, says verse 9: *You will break them* (the nations i.e. the pagans) *with a rod of iron.* In the same spirit one finds in Isaiah (63:3) the words: *I trod the nations in my anger, I trampled them in my fury, and their blood bespattered my garments.*

Many more such texts could be used to construct a Messianic image. It has even been suggested that volumes with collections of quotations from the Old Testament may have existed, which the Christians used as proof that Jesus was *the* Christ, as predicted by the prophets. Many see however, that the story about Jesus is mainly based on these Old Testament quotations, to which this story was made to conform. This process leads then to the creation of the image of the Jesus of the Gospels. This means, however, that only material leading to the creation of the image of a suffering Messiah was chosen from the sacred texts. The next chapter will examine how this process of selection and progressive construction might have developed. Here, the issue to be demonstrated is that the Messianic image encountered in the Gospels can be constructed out of the building blocks present in the Old Testament, as soon as the inner urges made this a necessity.

The people who were sensitive to these urges, the creators of such stories, were not so much individuals, rather they were groups. They could be described as communities, especially those in which the coming of God's reign was strongly anticipated, although there were maybe other groups who took part in this process. There were very many of them at the time, around the beginning of our era, mostly situated on the eastern boundaries of the Roman empire, even in the agricultural region near to the desert. It was there that the sect of the Essenes was founded, and where the disciples of John the Baptist, and others were found, or at least the centres of such beliefs were based there. Information about the Essenes is unambiguous, since the scrolls discovered give us much detailed information about their communal life.

Communities like these were searching diligently and earnestly for all that could give indications about the coming of the Messiah. Of course here too allegory played an important part. So it was important to stress that the Messiah will be the successor of Moses, because this Messiah was recognised also in Joshua. Philo wrote an extensive treatise on this, as we shall see later. Members of such a community would feel themselves members of a brotherhood called to achieve reconciliation before the end of time for the country, by scrutinising the Law and by living a holy and perfect life, separated from the world. They used no weapons and were capable, as already mentioned, of suffering with the utmost heroism, even accepting death. Death was laughed at because under the reign of the Messiah King a totally improved and happier era will dawn, if not for the individual, at least for the people with whom his or her group identifies.

The passion texts are not yet applied to the Messiah

The passion-texts were not yet applied to the Messiah. Nevertheless the faithful who gave their life for their faith are glorified. In the book "Wisdom of Solomon"(3:6) several of the faithful are mentioned, who are killed for their righteousness, which as the gift of a perfect sacrifice, is accepted by God. To be steadfast during persecutions one should be guided by Job and the Prophets. So, in this way, the Letter of James (5:10,11) does not mention anything to indicate knowledge of the history of the passion in the Gospel. In the same way the final Beatitude (Matt. 5:11,12) says: *Blessed are you, when you suffer insults and persecution and calumnies of every kind for my sake. Exult and be glad, for you have a rich reward in heaven; in the same way they persecuted the prophets before you.*

25

Those texts need to be isolated from the context in which they are placed and from the preacher who utters them in the Gospel. Such an aphorism may have been a well-known statement of 'Wisdom' personified.

What matters is that the prophets were known as martyrs for their faith. So people knew how to console each other with what was known about the suffering of a prophet like Jeremiah [see the chapters (Jer. 20:2, 37:16, 38:6-13) which describe Jeremiah put in the stocks, imprisoned and thrown into the pit]. They encouraged each other to follow the example of Daniel and his friends, who were thrown to the devouring beasts or in a furnace for the sake of their faith. Hebrews (11:32-38) gives an exhaustive summary of all those events, to strengthen the members of the community to steadfastness under persecution - apparently again without knowledge of the suffering Messiah.

But even when acquainted with this suffering or having heard of it from the history of the faithful, people did not apply the suffering for righteousness to the Messiah. Schürer, in his " Story of the Jewish people in the time of Jesus Christ" refers to 54 books dealing with the Messianic hope in Israel, but in none of them has there been found a trace of the reconciling suffering of the Messiah.

Nevertheless according to Justinus Martyr in his dialogue with Trypho, the Jews admit that prophecies like Isaiah 52 and 53 concern the suffering of the Messiah and that this one had to suffer. However, Schürer suggested that one has to assume that these Jews were brought to make these concessions in disputes with Christians. The representation of a suffering Messiah has been characteristic of some schools among the Jews, but it has never become the dominant opinion. The aspect of a suffering Messiah – and especially one who suffers to reconcile sins - first emerges in the communities of the early Christians.

Constructing the Messiah image of the Gospels

Birth of Jesus

That the image of the Messiah of the Gospels has been the result of a continuous process of reflection on the prophetic predictions as demonstrated above, appears clearly when attentively examining the Gospels. For reasons to be made clear later, the Gospel according to Matthew is chosen as an example here.

The Gospel begins with a genealogy of Jesus, son of Joseph who was of the lineage of David. Next follows the story of the birth of the same Jesus by the Holy Spirit and Mary. At this occasion the angel said to Joseph that he should call the child Jesus, because he will liberate the people from their sins. The name means 'God saves'. Matthew adds to this a second prophecy, from Isaiah 7:14 *The virgin will be pregnant and give birth to a son and he will be called Emmanuel.* Rather strange, these announcements, the second so closely following the first. These, however, are two names which people already knew as names for the coming Messiah. Next there follows the story of the slaughter of the infants in Bethlehem, because the prophet (Micha 5:1 and 3) had said: *You, Bethlehem, country of Judah, from you will come the one, who will care for Israel, my people* and because of the text: *A voice was heard in Ramah - - it is Rachel, who bewails her children, because they are no more there.* Then the Gospel writer places in between (mindful of Psalm 72:10 and 15: *May the kings of Tarshish and of the isles bring gifts* and: *May gifts of gold from Sheba be given him)* the story of the three kings from the east. This is also associated with Isaiah 60:6. *Camels in droves will cover the land, young camels from Midia and Eohah, laden with gold and frankincense* and also 49:7 *Kings will rise when they see you, princes will do homage.* Thus all has come to pass to confirm the predictions.

Baptism by John

The story continues with the appearance of John the Baptist, predicted, according to the Gospel writer, by Isaiah (40:3), with the words: *A voice crying in the wilderness: Prepare the way for the Lord; make straight in the desert a highway for him.* There follows the baptism by John. This last prophet and his actions are considered to be the end of Judaism, the summit so to speak, of the preaching: *The kingdom of God is near.* After this the curtain rises for the well-known story of the Saviour, especially when he receives the spirit with the words, borrowed from Isaiah (42;1) *Here is my servant, whom I uphold, my chosen one, in whom I take delight.* Three quotations from the Old Testament could also account for the story of the temptation in the desert: Deuteronomy 8:3, Psalm 91:11-12 and Deuteronomy 6:13.

The sayings, acts and miracles

Immediately after these temptations Jesus goes to Galilee and settles himself in Capernaum, because he had heard that John had been arrested. All this, according to the Gospel writer, because of the prophecy of Isaiah 9:2 about Galilee: - *The people that walks in darkness sees a great light.* This text was mentioned earlier, applied to the life and acts of the Messiah. Now the programme proper of Jesus' preaching follows: -*Repent, for the kingdom of Heaven is upon you* -, the message of John the Baptist, but this is soon interpreted in a broader sense. Then follows the calling of the first disciples, more or less inspired by the calling of Elisha by Elijah (Kgs. 19:21). Next the first healings, as expected, according the dominant theology, from the Messiah.

As for the Sermon on the Mount, it is generally assumed that no preacher could have produced this collection of linked proverbs, and that the sermon was put together by the Gospel writer from a number of proverbs, which he or his spokesmen attributed to Jesus. This could easily have happened, because visions and dreams were much valued. Often in these a word was addressed to the listener on behalf of God or the Messiah. The example of Paul on his way to Damascus demonstrates this clearly. Much of the material in the Sermon of the Mount stems from the Old Testament, allegorically explained of course, but there is also much from other sources. Allard Pierson (1878) gives a complete summary of all this. We are looking here, however, not so much for the words of Jesus, rather for his deeds and vicissitudes. There follow ten stories of miracles, from which in some cases it is evident that they have a metaphorical meaning; they describe the Son of God and his beneficent acting on the human soul. It was well known that the Messiah would perform such actions. In addition one can compare these miracles in some cases with some done by the prophets, in which case the story about Jesus is striking as it surpasses those Old Testament parables.

28

In Matthew 9 are found the words: - *Nor do people put new wine into old wineskins.* This he gives as an answer to the question why the disciples of John the Baptist had to fast whereas the disciples of Christ did not. Obviously it was a dispute between the group of followers of John and the Christians, as to why the latter had abolished the ritual law.

Twelve disciples were chosen, conforming to the number of tribes of the ancient people. To these Jesus addresses himself when sending them out into the world. It is clear that in this address all sort of instructions were given, stemming from the practice of the nascent Christianity in its relation to Orthodox Judaism. Antagonism had developed into an enmity between Orthodox Judaism and the Christians with the consequence that the Christian preachers were really sent out as sheep among wolves. Here, Jesus predicted some things; one may also say that many of these proverbs, inspired by contemporary practice, were put in the mouth of Christ as the supreme guide, here making use not of predictions but of material presented by common practice.

The invitation of Jesus: *Come to me... etc.* (Mat. 11:28) is a saying that can be thought of as spoken by the divine Wisdom or by the Logos, whose earthly appearance we find described in the Gospel. Jesus acts sometimes in secret – something which may be expected from the Messiah – and the Gospel writer therefore refers to the text Isaiah 42:2 *He will not shout or raise his voice, or make himself heard in the street.*

There follows, in Matthew 13, a series of parables which all refer to the Kingdom of God, as the first generations of Christians could experience this from day to day in the growth and the needs of their communities. There was a question, for instance, as to whether bad elements should be banished. There are places in the Gospels where this is defended but not here. Bad elements should be tolerated until the last day, the day of judgement. It is important to note, that the true meaning of these and other parables according the idea of the Gospel writer, is not accessible for every listener, but only for the chosen who are able to discern hidden truths, metaphorically expressed. It is even clearly stated that the Lord did not speak except in parables, according to Psalm 78:2: *I shall tell you a meaningful story; I shall expound the riddle of things past.* Therefore there are some few who understand the mysteries of the kingdom of heaven and many for whom this all passes by like a colourful story, of which the hidden meaning is not understood. It is a question of a higher knowledge of hidden truth, as found in the mysteries.

The Transfiguration on the mountain - Jesus alone, without either Moses or Elijah at his side - demonstrates that it is impossible to unite Christianity and Judaism (see also Chapter VII. p.53).

Here the writer takes sides in the debate with which Paul was confronted in his communities: whether to maintain the Jewish law, or not. The answer is not to maintain it. Therefore in Matthew 18 can be found all sorts of rules concerning community life, predicted by Jesus or put into his mouth. From Matthew 21 onward the Gospel gives the history of the passion. Here, more than anywhere, all has been made dependent on prophetic predictions: the entry into Jerusalem on a donkey (already mentioned), the purification of the temple, an illustration of the words of Jeremiah 7:11. Also on the prediction of the denial according to Zechariah (13:7); the prayer in Gethsemane (an excellent example of the struggle in praying that was expected from each Christian in dire circumstances (see also Psalm 43:5); the silence of Jesus facing Caiaphas according to Isaiah 53:7; the thirty pieces of silver as in Zechariah 11:12 and 13; finally the passion words and deeds proper, to be compared with Psalm 22:2 and 8, Psalm 69:22 and elsewhere.

This summary offers only the framework of the construction of the first Gospel. This would be filled up with all kinds of material, which will be treated later. The Gospel of Mark is constructed according to a similar pattern as well as that of Luke, though the latter has a quite distinctive character. They also indicate less clearly than Matthew from which sources their material is borrowed.

The prophesies and the life of Jesus

How can this correlation between prophecy, community experience and the Gospels be seen? There are three possibilities. First, by taking the standpoint of the orthodox churches of all subsequent centuries, accepting the supernatural and taking for granted that the prophets did indeed miraculously predict what later on would occur to Jesus and his community. Secondly, by taking a critical attitude towards the Gospel story and on that basis looking for the historical Jesus. Thirdly, by assuming that because the pattern of the Gospel story was, as mentioned earlier, to be found in the prophecies since ancient times, later generations simply embroidered on these. This implies that the Gospel story is a legend, lacking historical foundation.

As regards the supernatural conception and fulfilment, with, as annex, the many miracles narrated in the Gospel, God does not reveal himself in the supernatural but precisely in the natural. In our own era, we have learned to see natural miracles so great that, next to these, there seems no need for supernatural miracles. Taking a purely historical standpoint, the intervention by "miracles" can be excluded. This is not intended to attack the above-mentioned standpoint of the churches, but to leave it without further discussion.

As for the second position, by taking a critical stand and then looking for the historical Jesus totally objectively, not being guided by one's own cherished ideas about the rabbi of Nazareth, one comes to strange results. Schweitzer (1921) describes Jesus as a fanatic, who, disappointed in all his expectations concerning the end of the world, died on the cross a death without meaning. And those who want to correct this representation, based on Gospel data, will arrive at conclusions like H.B.Kossen's (1960). His standpoint is that Jesus intentionally followed all the prophecies, which he knew about since he was a boy. He would have followed step by step the indications and drew on these predictions. This point of view leads automatically to the image of an existence out of which all life and spontaneity disappeared. In this way Jesus becomes a sort of robot, a dummy, and an individual who is not acting on his own initiative but on external authority. Is it possible to imagine that the hero of the Gospel story therefore purified the temple with such ferocity because somewhere in the scriptures (Ps. 69:9) it was said: *Zeal for your house has consumed me*? Surely such a rambling and dependent person, could not have become an inspiring spiritual guide. Of course, it is possible, with many scholars, to attribute the references to ancient prophecies to the writers of the Gospels and after corrections for these aspects, to look for the historical figure that will remain. The construction and the style of the Gospels, however, resists this approach for the emphasis is explicitly laid on these elements and the intention is precisely to describe a supernatural person. See the books by Van den Bergh van Eysinga, "Jesus, does he live or has he only lived?" (1930) and "The nature of the Gospel history" (1939).

Jesus as a parable

The third point of view, that the Gospels don't describe historical events, but have to be understood symbolically, as parables, will be the basis of the next chapters.

CHAPTER V

Messianic Images

Several Messiah Images

The Christian image of the Messiah is known only from the Gospels. What is given is a person who is suffering love and who at the same time is also the image of God, represented in human form, as well as the image of the ideal human individual, who is a reflection of God. We will come back to this point later. But first it must be realized that there is not one such Messiah (Christ) image, but several. In the New Testament alone several Christ images are to be found, and this diversity becomes greater if consulting the non-canonic literature. Allard Pierson (1878) has put side by side as many as five Christ images. To mention only four of them: in addition to the synoptic Jesus there is the 'Lord' of Paul; next the incarnated Word of John and then the Christ of the Revelation. All these images are creations of a Judaism which was, here and there, already becoming Christianity with neither side realizing to what extent the one differed from the other.

Alexandria and surrounding Diaspora

Continuing to focus on the separation between the liberal Jews of Alexandria, including the further Diaspora on one side and the conservative Jews in Palestine on the other, hardly any traces of a more or less elaborated Messianic image can be found within the Alexandrian group. Josephus does not mention the figure of the Messiah, and Philo only occasionally. In those cases, this is more suggestive of compromises regarding the expectations of the people, than of the image of the Messiah being central in his thoughts, as

33

Müller (1870) demonstrates. This lack of reference may have been caused by striving to avoid making the pagans (who formed their main body of readers) uneasy with images. Such images could easily be understood as symbols of nationalist aspirations of the Jews (see Wilson op.cit. p.224) since Diaspora Jews, who were not in poverty and distress, were not in need of a nationalist symbol. Whereas the belief in a Messiah was more vivid in the lower popular classes than in the more philosophical, educated classes. In Philo's philosophy of religion two points and no more, are central: God and the human soul. Philo, therefore, does not recognise a holy history, in the sense that there is a need for a Saviour who brings redemption from human suffering. The redemption of the human person, he believes, is a psychological experience. When he meets such ideas on his journey through the Old Testament texts which could be called 'messianic', because in one way or another they hint at the coming redeemer, Philo spiritualises these in such a way that nothing remains but the mystical liberation of the soul, the only theme that matters for him. He doesn't see a future redemption but only a present one, inward, mystical one.

The Logos

However, Philo does know a mediator, not a man, but a celestial figure. This figure Philo places on the border between God and man, who mediates with God on behalf of men for forgiveness of their sins. He calls this figure the Logos, a concept which, as seen above, is from the philosophy of Plato. He makes this figure appear several times in human form. Among these forms in which the Logos incarnated, there is one which specifically interests him. He sees the Word of God, or God's spirit, specifically incarnated in Joshua, the ancient judge, successor of Moses as leader of the people. For this point and this person he has elaborate ideas. In his paper about 'the changing of names' he deals at length with the changing of the name Joshua, who was initially called Hozea, but according to Numbers (13:16) was re-baptised by Moses as Joshua, in Greek 'Jesus'. This name signifies, according to Philo, certainly not without some evidence, 'Salvation by God'. Now, this Jesus (Joshua) is the successor of Moses, "his most excellent disciple, inheritor of his loving character, and someone excellent in every respect". In the name of Yahweh, Moses appoints him, Joshua, as his successor. See Numbers 27:18: *Take 'Jesus' son of Nun, a man powerful in spirit, lay your hand on him* - One finds nearly the same in Deuteronomy 34:9: *And Joshua* (='Jesus') *was filled with the spirit of wisdom, for Moses had laid his hands on him.* Further, concerning this Joshua-Jesus in Exodus 33:11 - *The Lord used to speak with Moses face to face, as one man speaks to another. and Moses then returned to the camp, but his attendant, Joshua, son of Nun, never moved from inside the Tent.* Naturally the legend was woven around this event, that Joshua also spoke with God as one man speaks to another To this it can be added that Joshua did the most formidable miracle imaginable: he stopped the sun and the moon! Now this Joshua was in fact, according to Philo and his like-minded friends, a celestial figure - the Logos, incarnated in this exceptional man. Thus this Jesus-Joshua is the prototype of the Messiah Jesus, who will appear in the future. Just as Moses has been the mediator of the first covenant between God and man, so his later successor, Jesus, will be the mediator of the new covenant. In this way, one knows the name of the Saviour, at least if, as supposed in those circles, one disposes of the necessary gnosis (insight) to be able to understand such exegesis of the texts. Later generations, including Christians, often referred to the text Deuteronomy (18:15), Moses said: *The Lord your God will raise for you a prophet like me from among your own people; it is to him you must listen.* Origen[6] says of this: 'You will enter the promised land, into which, after Moses, Jesus will bring you and he will be your guide during the new journey'. Still another writer Eusebius[7] put it as follows: 'Jesus, the son of Nun, has been a reflection of our Saviour'. And still another, Justinus Martyr 'Jesus is a name of God, which was not known to Abraham or Jacob, but is pronounced by Moses in a mysterious way. Remember now, who introduced your ancestors in the new land; is it not exactly the same, who received the name Joshua, after first having been called Hozea?'. Allegorically it could be that Moses is the image of the powerful man who dominated men by the law of the first covenant, but that only through Jesus/Joshua, would the true believers be guided into the land of promise, the land of happiness, of inner freedom, the Kingdom of God; this is the man of the new covenant, as meant by Jeremiah in his prophecy (Jer. 31: 31-34). Thus is given, also for the liberal-minded Jews, a kind of Messianic teaching. However, this is quite different from that which we find elsewhere. That a celestial power, called Jesus, would bring to men true happiness, was however, already stated. Clearly related

35

to this Alexandrian theology is the way of thinking in the Letter to the Hebrews in the New Testament. The Christ is a celestial power, who acts like the true high priest in heaven. He is priest, 'according to the ordinance of Melchisedek', because his priesthood is ordained not according to the law, but according to the new covenant where the law is abolished. This letter does not suggest a Messiah image with traits of a more earthly character; here all is happening in heaven. The Gospel according to John also shows the traits of the Alexandrian Logos, especially clear in the prologue, but also apparent, more veiled, throughout the whole Gospel. Here, however this celestial figure is interwoven with traits borrowed from the synoptic tradition. All this corresponds more or less to the type of Christ which Pierson called the 'Christ-type of the incarnated Word' or the 'John type'.

The image of the national Messiah

The national Messiah image has a quite different character. This is most strongly present in the book of Revelation and comes nearer to the circle of ideas of the Jewish people in Palestine, though the image outlined there is not restricted to that country. The author of Revelation sees in a vision what will happen at the end of time. In this chaotic stream of fantasies he also sees Christ - or it may be better to say The Messiah, for a Jewish spirit is observable here in everything. This is someone who resembles a human child, with a long cloak and a golden girdle. At another place in the book of Revelation the Messiah appears like a rider on a white horse. Written on him was a name known to none but himself. A figure of a dignity greater than that of all kings. He was robed in a garment dyed in blood. Out of his mouth came a sharp sword to smite the nations, for it is he who will 'rule them with a rod of iron and tread the winepress of the fierce wrath of God, the sovereign Lord. On his robe and on his thigh was written the title: King of kings and Lord of lords. From other places in this book it becomes clear that it is the blood of the pagans that drips from the winepress'. This is a Messianic image, totally different from the synoptic Jesus, but also from the personified Logos discussed previously. This image is the product of the fantasy of a repressed and suffering people, expressing in this way all its hatred against its oppressors. An historical image of Jesus is absent here.

The Christ image of Paul

The Christ image of Paul assumes a special place. His Christ figure is composed of a future image of the judging Messiah and also one emerging from the past : The Lord who by his sacrifice has reconciled the faithful with God. This Christ as a mercy-mediating figure will be further examined in chapter VIII. As for the first aspect, Paul's expectations concerning the returning Christ are as vague as those of other apocalyptic scriptures. The future image is always limited to some outstanding traits and the rest remains in semi-obscurity. Thus it can be said of both Messiah images, the one of the past and the one of the future, that they contain hardly anything concrete. If we were not accustomed to reading the story of Jesus' life in the Gospels before we began to read the letters of Paul, the Saviour in those letters would make a similar impression to that of the saviours of the respective mystery cults of that time. An elaborate image of the Messiah does not emerge from these letters. In addition to all these Saviour figures it would also be possible to mention those outside the New Testament. For simplicity's sake we leave them out of this discussion.

The conventional Messiah image

Finally, there is the conventional Messianic image of the Jews, a somewhat vague figure of a Saviour to come, in which the idealised image of King David plays a big part. He will liberate the righteous – that means the Jews - from all enemies and take revenge on the sinners. In the book of Revelation this is strongly developed in a nationalistic way. This earlier vague image of an earthly king has later evolved into a heavenly figure, who is regarded more as saviour of the whole world.

The questions that remain

The questions that remain are:- Through which influences did the Jesus of the Gospels become the dominant of all those possible messianic images? How can this development be represented when the familiar representation of the life and the death of an historical Gospel hero is no longer available?

CHAPTER VI

The suffering Messiah

Introduction

If the current presentation of the Gospels (as a record of an historical event) is dropped, how did the familiar Messiah ideal of *the man of sorrows,* who suffered on the cross, develop? Or in other words: is it possible to imagine a course of history, other than the Gospel versions, that in the long run gave rise to the birth of Christianity?

Leaving aside, for a while, the development of philosophical ideas in the Diaspora, which will be dealt with later, first especially the more national popular belief will be examined.

The end of the national Messiah image

Differences between the Jewish and Christian image

To begin it will help to distinguish those aspects of the Christian Messiah ideal which differ from those of the Jewish ideal. In the first place there is the suffering. For the Jews the crucified Messiah is horrific and this will probably not change. Secondly, examining the transition from Judaism to Christianity, it should be noted that the Messiah of the Christians is a person out of the past, who has fulfilled the expectations of the faithful, at least in certain respects - whereas the Messiah of the Jews is a figure still in the future. So reversal has taken place from expectations projected in the future to a certainty of salvation based on the past. Thirdly, the central figure of Christianity is universal, aiming at the salvation of all men irrespective of frontiers or ritual rules. The Messiah of the Jews was and remains essentially a national figure strictly associated with a particular people. Fourthly, the Christian Saviour has come to save all men from sin whereas the Jewish Messiah will come to save a particular people from oppression and suffering.

Considering the literature of the first century, it becomes clear that a suffering Messiah is not mentioned earlier than in the Christian literature. This Christian literature, primarily the Gospels, was written, according to careful estimates, in the years between 70 and 100 CE – some scolars date them even later. Their dating is usually assumed to be as follows: first Mark, between 70 and 80, then Matthew between 80 and 90, and finally Luke between 90 and 100. Of course these dates should not be taken too strictly but indicate the time when the life-histories of Jesus were put on record, or at least when their foundation was laid. There followed a long period, during which additions were still made or in some way or another the content was modified. Evidently Christian literature began after the end of Israel's existence as an independent nation. Until then there was no question of a Christian literature with a suffering and crucified Jesus.

The destruction of the Temple

In the year 70 CE the independent national existence of the Jewish people in Palestine came to an end with the destruction of the town of Jerusalem and the temple in its midst. We encounter this tragic year regularly in the history of the Church of the first century, probably without sufficiently realising the immense significance which this event had in the conceptual world of the Jews of that time. For long Judaism had occupied an important place in the Roman empire and the Temple was of such interest that the emperor Titus, who finally took the city, wanted to save it, if at all possible, not least for the immense riches it contained. In the end this plan failed, because a Roman soldier threw a burning torch into the inner part of the temple. When the flame blazed out from the most sacred sanctuary a scream of despair escaped from the few surviving Jews, trying to defend their sanctuary to the very last moment against the hated foreigners. For – and this should also clearly be realised – the siege was accompanied by starvation, because the Romans were not able to capture the strong fortress without it and as a consequence about a million people had perished. During the siege a tremendous fanaticism prevailed in this multitude, though they were divided in factions, sharply fighting each other! Only when the siege became a serious threat did the fighting groups become united. They believed unshakeably that God would not abandon his city and his temple. When the Jewish historian Flavius Josephus (who was in the Roman army camp, because he was taken prisoner and had chosen the Roman side) by order of the emperor called out to his fellow citizens that they should surrender, they shouted to him: 'Jerusalem can never be conquered, because she is the holy city of God'. They believed that hosts of angels, whether or not under the command of the Messiah, would come to rescue the city. All this while women were already eating the flesh of their children! Something of this mood is encountered in the message of Revelation (11:1- 6). Here, the fate of the besieged Jerusalem is described. It will be trampled down during forty-two months by the Gentiles, but, while they profane even the porch of the temple, its most inner part will be saved by a miracle, because two witnesses of God, Moses and Elijah, will act. They are able to consume everyone who threatens them or the temple by the fire that comes out of their mouths. Those who had based their hopes on this were, however, disappointed. As were all others who had based their expectation on the coming of the Messiah.

The impression made by the fall of the city and the temple should not be underestimated. It may be true that a large and important part of Jewry consisted of Jews in the Diaspora, who were not physically confronted with this disaster, but still they felt united with the Palestinian Jews by their veneration of the holy city. Because of the war with Rome, the relations between Jews and pagans in the other places where Jews were living also became disturbed, with the consequence that these Jews had to suffer quite a lot themselves. Even when Judaism did not perish after this disaster, thanks to the synagogues established everywhere, nevertheless the fall of the city and even more the destruction of the temple was a traumatic event of world order, especially for the Jews in the Roman empire.

Reaction to the destruction of the temple

Now the question arises: How would their religious consciousness have reacted or responded to the tragedy of this fall? Three possibilities seem likely here:

First, as a result of being totally broken by the definitive failure of all they had ever hoped for and expected, they might loose their faith. There must have been many such, who naturally disappeared from history, because they would have denied their nationality and would have become assimilated into the surrounding culture. No more can be said about them.

Secondly, in contrast to these some might adopt an attitude of protest and isolate themselves in their own centuries-old religious scriptures and traditions. Many did so, following the example of the rabbis who, when they happened not to live in Jerusalem at the time of the disaster, continued, undisturbed, to weave their webs of exegesis. Thus there remains, in different forms and colours varying by time and country of settlement, the attitude of the Law-abiding Jews up to this day.

The third attitude is neither a resentful protest, nor the hardening indifference towards destiny, but acceptance of this sorrow from the hand of God. On examination this attitude appears strictly opposed to the rigidly national one. Those accepting would have to endure the reproach of those taking the latter that they haven't been sufficiently nationalist, especially by neglecting the Law, as was the case for many, especially in the Diaspora. They are thus to blame as the cause of the past disasters. On the other hand, the thought lived in this more patient party, that God had inflicted this punishment for the arrogance of his chosen people. So, in these circles, the first consequence of this loss of national existence was that they realized that the national expectation has to be changed fundamentally. The national Messiah fell off his pedestal.

The origin of the image of a suffering Messiah

Palestinian Judaism also submerged in religious syncretism

Here there needs to be a pause, for at this moment in history the scene changed; a change which merits careful analysis. Until this time two streams of thought are discernible: one that of the old Jewish homeland with its Messiah ideal, the other of the Diaspora with its Logos teaching and allegorizing. This is about to change. The Diaspora Jews had already been confronted, and this during a rather long time, with the whole spectrum of influences in the empire. Although Palestinian Jews were not totally unaffected by this process, they were capable of resisting it far more effectively than their relatives in foreign countries. After the end of Israel's national existence this became more difficult. Indeed, faith in being the so-called chosen people was now also lacking. It was this faith that in the past had united the compatriots throughout the empire. It can be seen, however, that after the year 70, this conservative part of Jewish ideas and thoughts finally also became submerged in the turmoil of religious and philosophical ideas, which at that time asserted themselves everywhere. Now, for the first time, Judaism is subject to that syncretic movement where everything – with or without allegorizing – is related to everything, and where the historian loses his way in the multitude of sects and schools with barely known names. This process of syncretism becomes even more complicated because of the changed combinations of the players on this scene. Whereas until this time it was the Jews themselves who produced the changing flow of ideas, this now alters: the proselytes or 'God-fearing' (those pagans who adhered to the Jewish synagogue without fulfilling the Law completely) began to play a leading role, while the more liberal Jews fused more and more into those circles. It is clear these newcomers brought with them much of the teaching and the spirit of the circles from which they came, among them the Stoics and other schools of wisdom already mentioned.

However, while earlier those ideas influenced only the Jews in the Diaspora, now the whole of Jewry was affected. Where, in this turmoil of ideas, all was mixed, the Logos-wisdom and the idea of a messiah became amalgamated. Jewish and Greek ideas were in a melting process, in which the composing elements can be retraced only with difficulty. A new type of religion arose. Here we find the cradle of Christianity, though the moment when it would be called by that name was still far away. The movement continued for a long time as an extreme but associated branch of Judaism, until events in which both sides recognised the essential differences forced a split. Friedländer (1898) speaks, in this context, of a certain kind of Jewish gnosticism which in the long run became Christianity.

Suffering as a metaphysical necessity

The decline of the Jewish nation, and with it the Jewish religion, brought, among the more liberal groups of Jews and their

42

proselytes, the universalists thought that finally the whole world is the homeland of all men, at least of the wise. Related to this, the thought that even for a nation suffering can become a vocation! The Logos-teaching now became connected with this. For a long time it had been taught, in the line of Philo, that the Logos as the representative of God or as the personal image of His spirit, had lived in the people of the Law and had led this people through all their tribulations. This spirit - symbolically speaking, perished with the nation - had died only to be resurrected in another form, when a new community would have arisen. As long as this new community was not yet visible for every one, no attention was given to this last thought. One limited oneself to expressing one's belief in a suffering Logos: God has to suffer as soon as he shows himself incarnate in the world. This is the leading idea of the Gospel of John, that the light shines in the darkness but is not understood. It was, therefore, fought and treated with hostility. Where the Word becomes flesh – in the prophets, the community of the people – it cannot be understood by the blind, ignorant world and is therefore hated by the world. The same will be the case with other bearers of this divine Word of Wisdom, its followers will be persecuted and killed, out of ignorance. Here the suffering of the faithful is seen as a metaphysical necessity. This Wisdom, wishing to spiritualize all things, and therefore striving to bring all existing religions into a deep mystical experience, and in doing so undermining those religions, will be doubly hated. These things are made clear in epic form, when the divine Logos in the person of Christ, is purifying the temple, adding to this that he, the Logos, will demolish this human-built temple and rebuild it in three days:- the resurrection of the community. That this Wisdom is not understood, leads in the story - which is one continuous parable of the works of God's spirit in this world - to the death by crucifixion. But as it happens to the hero of the Gospels, it will happen to his followers (read 'the followers of the divine Wisdom'). They will find the world against them. Hence the words: *He who loves me, let him take up his cross and follow me.* Such thoughts and representations are entirely born out in their life experience, as much in that of the Jews as of the Greeks. Here and there they caused a letting go of all forms, with the consequence that religion became totally integrated into a philosophy of life, a vision that would mean the end of both the religious development and of the philosophy. Friedländer, in his Apologetik, especially Ch. VIII, tells us a lot about the hostile attitude of those rabbis loyal to the Law towards these emancipated compatriots; implying the persecution of one group by the other. From the Greeks, we know of the continuing influence of Plato, who lets Socrates say that to inflict injustice is worse than to suffer injustice. There are many more passages that could be cited to demonstrate the general mood in the philosophical circles of the first century CE.

The Messiah idea is changing

All these determinants together lead to the result that in emancipated Jewish circles the Messiah ideal was changing. Indeed, a quite new spirit arose, which would continue, transmuting into Christianity. Thus as stated above, future expectations changed from nation-oriented to become more universal.

As we have seen, in the circles of the allegorists like Philo, the idea of salvation in the future was spiritualised into present salvation in the spirit :- *parousis* came to mean the advent of the Messiah, of the Christ in the spirit and the promised land as the possession of the secret truth. The Lord is the Spirit, Paul says, and this idea will not have lived only in him. Indeed, often, where the Gospels speak of an impure spirit that has to be banished, one should interpret this as the need for healing from excessive nationalism. The liberating spiritual power, or whatever one may call this, no longer liberates from oppression, but from sin. Hence Matthew (**1:21**) *for he will save his people from their sins*. The Messiah ideal itself will come to conform to this idea. In the circles of the patient the idea of a future victory over the pagans was given up for universalism, where one's own people had to be at the service of mankind, where the old Messiah ideal was altogether pushed aside, where they comforted each other with figures like Job and the prophets as innocent pious sufferers. There, the Messiah figure had to reach still higher and had to take on a martyr character, a refuge for people in need and distress, a help to raise oneself again. This figure, too, is found in the scriptures, seen in the text at Luke (**24:44ff**). There the resurrected Lord says to the travellers on the road to Emmaus who had lost every hope: *Everything written about me in the law of*

44

Moses and the prophets and the psalms must be fulfilled. Then he opened
their minds to understand the scriptures.

The mystic garment of this story can now be left for what it is,
only concluding that at that time the texts of the old testament were
scrutinized in search of traits of the suffering Messiah. The issue
at stake here is the allegorical interpretation of those old texts, for
which the mind had to be opened by means of special divine illu-
mination. In this way the suffering community created out of its
own needs its Messiah image, for here also the inner feelings were
responsible for the process of selection of the respective relevant
traits. This process was totally intuitive, not analytical, as is our
description here. Nevertheless it has been necessary to analyse it,
in order to understand it.

It was, therefore, not the Lord who created the community, but
the community who gave birth to this Lord out of its own religious
needs. Even this way of putting it is still too rational, approached
too much from the outside. The truth is that the one and the other
developed simultaneously. The figure of the Lord as Saviour devel-
ops in and with the community, which on the other hand finds its
unity precisely in this figure. A simple identification naturally takes
place between a confessional group, a group of believers, and the
object of their veneration, the figure in which they recognise their
ideal.

Thus out of the thoughts and emotions of this martyred
community, the image of the arch martyr, Jesus, is born. When this
image, as a sort of archetype, became rooted in the soul it was developed by scrutinising the scriptures of the old testament.

We have already mentioned a number of texts, but add that
those texts did not come really to life until the Christian community, through their own suffering, brought them to life.

The suffering servant of the Lord

The following presents the image of the suffering servant of the
Lord, in Isaiah (52:13, 53:12), in which the community recognises
itself and its Messiah:

He had no form or comeliness, he was despised and rejected by men;
a man of sorrows and acquainted with grief and as one from whom

men hide their faces. Surely he has borne our griefs and carried our sorrows. . . He was wounded for our transgressions, he was bruised for our iniquities; upon him was the chastiment that made us whole, and with his stripes we are healed. We, like sheep have gone astray; we have turned every one to his own way and the Lord has laid on him the iniquity of us all. He was oppressed and he was afflicted, yet he opened not his mouth; like a lamb that is led to the slaughter, and like a sheep, that before its shearers is dumb, he opened not his mouth.... Yet when he makes of himself an offering for sin, he shall see his offspring, he shall prolong his days; the will of the Lord shall prosper in his hands; he shall see the fruit of the travail of his soul and be satisfied; by his knowledge shall the righteous one, my servant, make many to be accounted righteous.

It is quite understandable that a martyred community recognised itself and its Lord in this picture. Many passages from these chapters play a part in the Passion story of the Gospels. One can also know from this text what God's purpose was in the toilsome life of that ancient people or that ancient leader, for by the wisdom of this servant of God many will be made righteous.

The suffering, also the suffering of the community, has a purpose as a substitute sacrifice for others, who are the real offenders. He who accepts this freely will find in it his comfort. So the suffering figure of Christ took the place of the warlike Messiah, but at the same time the figure of the future was replaced by the figure from the past. What had the suffering community to hope for? In fact it had given up all expectations, little by little letting them vanish. Indeed, none of these hopes were realised. Therefore it can be said that Church history of the first century was a process of continuing de-eschatologising: the *parousis* (the coming of the Messiah) and the coming of the thousand-year empire connected with it, were postponed to a far away future, and, in practice ceased to play an important role in the faith. Instead came the Lord who had suffered and who could therefore be a saviour for his community in their religious struggle.,

Résumé

To resume what has been said in this chapter, the following thesis can be proposed:

46

The suffering Christ is a figure created by the poetical imagination of the suffering community as a symbol of this suffering. Next: - this symbol will have a more vigorous effect on the religious complexion than an historical personality, because it was born out of the soul of men and adapted to their needs.

Therefore the Christ has not been reasoned away, but on the contrary, made inwardly alive for the faithful heart, a force within that will expresses itself quite naturally in an outward attitude.

CHAPTER VII

The Lord who rises with his community

The community of the New Alliance: a characteristic

That the Lord, God's representative, who would appear at the end of time and should have to suffer to rise again, had been revealed to the seers, the believers in the new alliance, others stayed blind to the truth. To the believers it was also revealed that the Lord had suffered; the where and when not yet being clear. From these believers, who saw the old in a new light and read the Old Testament as one on-going allegory, which they alone could understand, quite naturally a new community was born, the new alliance.

The Sabbath was not longer seen as an outward rest from the daily work. but as a symbol of that heavenly peace which God promised to the faithful. So the letter to the Hebrews states: *So then, there remains a Sabbath rest for the people of God.* The precepts for cleanliness do not actually mean the observable cleanliness, as it was understood by the ancients, but inner pureness of the heart, of the spirit. So circumcision is no more than the shadow of the real circumcision, i.e. the purification of the soul. As for healing – the Holy Ghost who inspired the old scriptures, does not mean corporal healings, but spiritual ones, which are much more precious. When one speaks of resurrection, this is not an event that, previously unforeseen, will take place in the future, but a metamorphosis out of a life of sin into a God-worthy life. When one thinks of the Messiah, then it is not in fact of a human being, but of the spirit personalised in a human form. The spirit which as the spirit of truth always has to suffer in a world of untruthfulness, and which therefore suffers in his followers, in the suffering community, is symbolically expressed in its 'body'.

These things need to be very clearly understood. Spiritualization has already been mentioned above and in this context the new congregations spiritualised the old values, laws and truths. This term is acceptable, provided that 'spiritualization' does not mean a degree of abstraction such that all concrete sense is lacking. That would not be true. For the *spiritual* Sabbath is a spiritual rest, a peace. It is of a higher order:- pureness of heart, mind or soul is not simply a word that evaporates without meaning, but a reality to be experienced. Spiritualizing of healings does not take away their sense, but bestows on them a deeper significance. Again this is a reality for those who have experienced it. The same holds true for the Messiah who, although also spiritualised, is unimaginable as such without the concrete congregation as the bearer of the spirit. Here we are dealing with realities of a higher order, no less real than the observable reality outside. Therefore instead of spiritualization one could say rather: 'seeing these religious things as symbols, in fact as a process of allegorizing'.

The community as the 'body of the Lord'

This idea of 'concrete spiritualization' can be elaborated a little further, especially in relation to the congregation as the 'body of the Lord'. Such ideas are not exclusively Christian. Although Paul speaks several times of the congregation as the temple of God, he was not the first to do so.

Furthermore 'temple' is not 'body'. Already Philo and with him other Alexandrians had such ideas. With the understanding that each temple, however impressive and beautiful it may be, is still unworthy of God, comes the thought that it is in the human heart that the invisible deity dwells.

God descends into the human heart and by that man is lifted up to God. 'That is pure Alexandrian- Jewish- religion-philosophy', Friedländer says, to which he adds a saying of Philo: 'Where God is moving invisibly into our soul to dwell there, we want to make it as worthy of Him as possible. The house most worthy of

God is the noble soul' (*De Cherub I:157*). Of course the consequence of this is that men have to live as purely as possible to keep God's dwelling free from corruption by the outside world. Paul expresses this in an identical way. The same ideas are expressed several times in Barnabas (16:9): 'It is God himself who prophesies in us. He himself dwells in us'. So the congregation is composed of the bearers of the spirit; that is to say, of men who have discovered the truth behind appearances, and it is precisely in this spirit that the presence of the Lord of the congregation is found. The Lord and his congregation form a mystical unity; they are in a certain way identical. Paul expresses this same idea with the words: *The church is the body of Christ.* That is to say, He dwells there as spirit. (See Galatians 1:24, 1 Corinthians 12:27, 6:19).

The Lord rises with his community

The same holds true for the resurrection idea: the Lord rises together with his community. This community rises as soon as the members of this new Church see themselves as such. For quite a long time they had considered themselves as radical Jews, just as they were considered by the Jewish community, so radical that they denied the Law yet still linked with the people of the old religion, which was itself in a process of fermentation. However, in every town where there was a synagogue, an assembly could be found who shared identical ideas, people that in the long run were striving for things quite other than those of their previous allegiance. Then arose the idea of the new community which is shaping itself out of the old one, the 'Church of God' is reborn in a new form. This process is intuitively transferred to the Lord of the community.

This Lord, the representative of God, the Son of God (at that time a quite common colloquial expression) was present and active as an inspiring spirit in the prophets, in Moses and in a sense in the people of the Law as a whole. This people died and with it also the Lord, whose name, following a holy tradition, should be Jesus. Then, when a new community regenerates out of the old, quite naturally the belief arises that the spiritual Lord is risen too. Soon the legend takes it up as a story, investing it with miracles.

According to legend the Lord himself had predicted these things. When he was asked to do miracles he answered: 'I will demolish this temple and after three days rebuild it'. 'What else could he have meant by this temple than the community which had first to be destroyed, then to be restored in visible form?' – so they teach one another. If the community is his body in a concrete form, in which the spirit lives and works, then his body that had to suffer and died, revives in a new form, in fact he revives himself. The Lord resurrects with and within his community. This community is now the true spiritual Israel and, at the same time, God's temple for the new era.

The spirit in that community - previously in the people - incarnates again and again. Indeed, true gnostics, who possess the necessary insight, go still further and identify this idea with that of the *parousis*, the coming of Christ, the long dreamed-of Messiah, and even with the pouring out of the holy Spirit, which becomes one with the community in which it has chosen to live. In any case, the resurrection of Jesus coincides with the resurrection of the Christians as a spiritual revival recurring again and again after suffering and death.

Onset of the severing process from Judaism

The Palestinian rabbinate mounts guard

The Palestinian rabbinate, the Scribes and the Pharisees came to the same conclusion: - 'here is a new religion, which despises our law and preaches salvation which for us Jews has a totally alien sense'. Gradually the Jewish clergy began to define its attitude and to mount guard around the sanctuaries venerated from ancient times. Accusations arose. In addition burgeoning Christianity was not the only liberal sect to cause difficulties for the Jewish leaders. Friedländer mentions repeatedly the sharp, nearly hopeless fight of the rabbis with the so-called Minim.[8] It has been assumed that this term referred to Christians, but it is not as simple as that, because many different groups of gnostics existed, even among the Jews. These are difficult to distinguish from each other and among them were some with very strange heresies. Even if his Minim could not simply be identified as Christians, the latter surely belonged in this category, at least when Friedlander claims that 'Minim means antinomous gnostic'. Between the Minim and their adherents on one side and the party of the conservative Jews, loyal to the law, on the other the dispute was very virulent. These 'modern liberals' overwhelmed the rabbis with their allegorical insights and wisdom. The latter were attacked so vehemently, that they often could not parry the arguments, finding no other solution than to retreat more and more rigidly into their body of laws and exegesis, to close ranks more tightly. Meanwhile accusations were raining reciprocally, which can be retraced in the Talmud and the resonance of which registers in the Gospels.

The best example of this may be the accusation which was formulated against Stephen by the Jewish high court. This states: *This man never ceases to speak words against the holy place and the law; for we have heard him say that this Jesus of Nazareth will destroy this place, and will change the customs which Moses delivered to us* (Acts 6:12). Clearly this was the same accusation with which Jesus was charged when confronting Caiaphas: *This man has said 'I am able to destroy the temple of God and to build it in three days'. (*Matt. 26:61) This has been called a false accusation, but in fact it reflects very clearly the objections of the conservative Jews to dissolution of the law and liturgy, that is to say 'other morals', among those of the new spirit. Many such accusations by Jews against Christians can be found in the Gospels, in addition to banishment from the synagogues, trials before judges and many other persecutions.

Anti-Jewish passages in the Gospels

The attack of Jesus on the temple, at the beginning of the short period of his activities in Jerusalem, can be seen as the symbolic summary of the attack by Christianity on Judaism, making understandable the accusations. The young community does not hesitate to reply and the Gospels contain a great number of anti-Jewish statements, parables and stories. To make a complete list becomes difficult, especially once alerted to the symbolic sense behind the words. There are many sensitive bible-readers can discover for themselves. When Jesus does not consider the fasting of his disciples as necessary, this amounts to the dissolution of the law in this context, clearly anti Jewish. The same is true when he does not observe the Sabbath with the same strictness as conservative Jews.

During the transfiguration on the mountain, of the three great figures: Moses, Elias and Jesus, only Jesus is left and a voice is heard: *This is my beloved Son in whom I take delight: listen to him* (Matt.17:5): clearly anti Jewish. The tenants in the vineyard, the Jews in the promised land, chase all those who were sent to collect the rent - the good deeds the Lord wants to see; finally they kill the son of the Lord, who gives the vineyard to other tenants. This story refers of course to the conquest of the land in and after 70 CE. It is considered as punishment for the rejection by the Jews of Christianity, personalised by Jesus.

Judas

The figure of Judas, the traitor, or as it is sometimes translated 'the one who delivers', has to be referred to in this context. The entry and development of this character in the Gospels is closely related to the development of the relation between the Jews and the young Christian churches. Judas is absent in the oldest fragments of the New Testament. In Corinthians(I:15:5) there is talk of twelve apostles, as was probably already the case in the hypothetical lost script on which our Gospels are based. In Matthew (19:28) twelve thrones are promised to the apostles so probably this story also did not know of a traitor. Neither Peter in his letters, nor Clemens, nor Ignatius, mention the traitor. This suggests that not until the time that Judaism had really 'betrayed' or 'delivered' Christianity (see Ch.VIII) was the figure of Judas created, as a personification of the Jews in the poetical imagination of the young community. See also of the words of Stephen in his speech (Acts 7:52) where he speaks of Jesus as the righteous one *whom you have now betrayed and murdered"*. Finally, the name Judas seems to refers to Judaei, the Jews.

Anti-Jewish parables

The same anti Jewish spirit is evident in several parables. There is the fig tree that withers: a symbol of withering Judaism, at least as it was seen by the Christians of that time. There are the two sons, the yes-saying one and the no-saying one. The first is pious in words but without deeds, the second looks impious, because he does not acknowledge liturgy in the sense of Judaism, therefore ignores the service of the word, but finally he does more than his yes-saying brother. This no-saying brother is paganism. When a Lord wishes to have guests at his wedding dinner but none of those invited come, refusing with all sort of excuses, the Lord at last invites beggars from the streets, then again paganism and Judaism are contrasted in such a way that the latter show the dark side of the coin.

In the Gospel according to Luke, already more favourable to the pagans, there is the parable of the merciful Samaritan. Here again the Jews play the unfavourable parts. The same is the case in the parable of the lost son, where the unfavourable role is attributed to the eldest son.

It would be possible to continue, but two examples from the Gospel according to John must suffice. Lazarus is resurrected; he is the symbol of paganism. In Canaan the watered wine of Judaism is replaced by the good wine of Christianity.

In all these Gospel stories we can see, as it were, the relationship between Jews and Christians getting gradually worse. The accusation from the Christian side comes to a climax when Paul, in the first letter to the Thessalonians (I:2:14,16), writes: ... *the Jews, who killed the Lord Jesus and the prophets .... now retribution has overtaken them for good and all.* They are punished by losing their country and their holy city.[9] This destruction seems to confirm that this radical, mystical, emancipated, new community is right: this is the end predicted by the prophets!

Not the victory in glory of the Jewish people but the end of this people and the beginning of a new people, the true Israel, the heavenly Jerusalem.

All this implies a definite severing of Christianity from Judaism, the developing independence of the resurrected community of the New Alliance. The Christian church emerges as such when the Jewish Synagogue finally takes measures to deal with the new situation.

Thus it is clear that in the beginning it was not the Gospel that created the community, but the community, out of its religious needs, that created the Gospel.

CHAPTER VIII

The new faith

The impact of the mystery religions

A community of pagan Christians

The centre of gravity of the community shifted more and more to the Greek-speaking converts. This Hellenist influence continued after the definite split from Judaism. Data about this are difficult to obtain. However, it seems quite natural that within the new church the existing minority of Jews would become weaker, because some of them, perhaps contrary to their preference, still maintained their allegiance to Judaism. The new growth of the community must have come mainly from pagans. If this is correct, then the new community after a short time would have become a community of pagan Christians, who as already stated, brought still more of their own ideas with them into the community. It is not adequate to call this 'treachery of the true teaching': they simply could not react in any other way and interpreted via their own understanding and in their own forms the 'truths' being preached. Thus in the community many things appear in a different light. Most of these proselytes would have been recruited from the religious circles of the many mystery religions of that time. The well-known authors, Reitzenstein, Wendland, Gaston Boissier and Cumont give important descriptions of the outstanding characteristics of these religious forms.

The general need for redemption

There follows a short overview, following H. Wagenvoort in his well-known work "The Religions of the World", more specifically in the chapter concerning the religion of the Greeks, here and there complemented with data from elsewhere. He starts from the need for redemption, which was at that time rather general. This need had different motives: some were looking for redemption from the transitory nature of the earthly life, others saw this terrestrial life as totally imprisoned in matter, seen as sinful as compared to the higher, spiritual reality. Next there was the need to be redeemed from guilt, which in its origins was still of a cosmic nature. There was a seeking for liberation from destiny, perceived as the influence of the stars as an inexorable power over human life.

H. Jonas (1954) writes of this in terms of the philosophy of Heidegger. Jonas speaks of the feeling of 'being thrown' into a meaningless world, and the anguish, the nostalgia and the feeling of being lost which accompanies this, providing the reason to escape into the inner life. Hence the introversion characteristic of this period.

Another relation with the deity

Clearly all those mystery religions preached a merciful God, present to help men in need. This was a very different conception of the deity from that held until this time by most people, even among the Jews. The priests of the mystery cults claimed that they possessed a secret wisdom which could be the key for the blissful life being sought. In order to arrive at this state of beatitude one had to obtain and respect knowledge about the rites and sacraments. Beside the idea of a God who had come from heaven, and sometimes woven into it – not always reciprocally related in a logical way – was the idea of a dying and resurrecting God. Sometimes this was a female, a Goddess. To be sure this cult had developed out of the veneration of nature, repeatedly dying and regaining fertility afterwards, the earth as Mother-Goddess. The destiny of this God/Goddess was represented by a drama, a Passion play, where the myth, the story about the vicissitudes, functioned as explanation of this drama. The initiate had himself to experience this suffering and dying of the divinity, not only by looking but by identifying with the god, often by himself going through initiating rituals, which seemed to be a deadly threat, out of which unexpectedly he was freed to a new life. This form served especially to convince the faithful of the revival of the soul after earthly death. It was quite natural that here, too, things were spiritualized. This scheme of death and resurrection was soon applied to liberation from the moral death of an earthly, sinful life.

All sorts of rituals served to give more depth to these different aspects: the dying of the God was loudly bewailed, his revival applauded equally loudly. However, the disclosure of these rituals was severely punished, surely mainly because those who did not have a sufficiently maturity, who had not seen the truth with an inner eye, would not be able to recognize the scenes as symbols of their own inner life and would be likely to take them to be ridiculous or offensive.

Based on an obligatory solemn oath of secrecy, a community of initiates developed a totally different character from other religious communities, and a strong and intriguing attraction for outsiders, due to the secrecy of their solemn mysteries. Some elements of this esoteric character have found their way into Christianity, as seen in expressions like: 'He who hath ears to hear, let him hear'.

Other important traits

There were other traits of these mystery-communities which are important here. Whereas the earlier community forms focused more on the salvation of the group, a more individual need for salvation moved into the foreground. In all mysteries the first aim was personal immortality or a blessed life in the hereafter; death and resurrection being seen as the contrast between the life on earth and the future life of the soul. Salvation was then also seen as personal, not as something regarding the community. There was a common meal, that belonged to the secret rituals, where the initiate not only communicates with others, but also shares in the essence of the divine. The priest was thought to be the mediator for the salvation sought. In the community of the chosen ones all ranks, classes, races or differences between people were eliminated. There was no question of excluding slaves and women. In these communities they took as worthy a place as men and were as important. There were degrees of initiation and whoever reached the highest degree dedicated him- or herself so intimately to the deity, that this tie is compared with the bond of marriage.

The ambiguity of Paul: Jesus as judge and as redeemer

To return now to Paul, whose theology is more or less ambiguous. On one side there is talk of the future coming of Christ, on the other hand the Christ has appeared already as the merciful redeemer. Attempts have been made to reconcile both these viewpoints by speaking of the return of Christ as the judge. Judging, after he lived on earth preaching forgiveness and mercy. However, the word used to refer to the coming of Christ, *parousis*, does not mean return, but simply arrival. This is the reversal, described above, of the belief in a future saviour or judge into a saviour who has appeared already as the suffering Lord, who brings the sacrifice of his life for the sins of men. This can be recognised in the difficulty of reconciling both and the endeavours to relate them.

Attention has already been drawn to the first aspect, the coming of Christ in the very near future, in relation to the abolition of Jewish Law, which would lose its validity when the Messiah arrived. Since, for Paul, the Messiah was already knocking on the door of the world, the abolition of Jewish Law seemed justified.

As for that other aspect, the arrival of the Messiah in the past, as Redeemer, it recalls the liberation ideas of the mystery religions. It is, as it were, its reflection in the Jewish spirit.

The general pessimism

In relation to the strong need for liberation in those days in pagan circles H.Jonas was mentioned above, as one of those who emphasises the pessimism of that time. This pessimistic mood was rather general. Seneca, for one, goes very deeply into it. He declares that the desire for wrong is inborn in every man: all sins hide in all, even when they are not manifest in every individual (*De Ira* 31.8 and IV: 27.3). He further declares that one should not so much concentrate on specific sins, but more generally on sinfulness (*Epistulae* 29,8; *De Ira* II 28, 1-3). Moral improvement for him is not enough: one cannot reach perfection step by step but only by a total change, which he calls *transfiguration* (Seneca, *Epistulae* 6;1), a concept re-encountered in the letters of Paul as metamorphosis. By one's own force one cannot surmount one's foolishness and weakness. Someone has to offer a helping hand to pull one out of it. (*Epistulae* 52, 1), therefore a divine man or a human god is needed.

Deep reflection on the general sinfulness of man can be found, too, on looking for these ideas in the Jewish context. Mostly such thoughts were considered there in relation to the story of the Fall and they led to the conclusion that no man, born of woman, exists who does not sin. Since. on the other hand, every man remains responsible for his own sin, it was said: 'Everyone has become an Adam for himself'. Furthermore, as God cannot remit the punishment for this sin, a mood of severe expiation dominates in these circles. So here, too, there exists a profound pessimism based on the general sinfulness of the human race (see also: Bertholet). All these pessimistic ideas are met again in Paul, especially in the Letter to the Romans (1:18-3:20). Obviously he is only one of the representatives of the general climate of that time. This general need for redemption is, in Paul, coupled with the belief in a deity who saves man from his distress. This part of the theology of Paul is accounted for by the general historical situation.

So, clearly, there exists a significant relationship between this Pauline Christianity and the religious mood of the mystery cults. It must have been the new members of the community going over from these mystery cults who stitched this new piece of cloth onto the old garment of Christianity, which still had a Jewish character. In the letters of Paul the seam remains visible.

Elements borrowed from the mystery cults

Christian authors, of course, have always attributed this relationship to a satanic imitation of Christian forms. It is more likely, however, those belonging to the mystery cults were right in conversely reproaching the Christians for having borrowed these things uncritically from the older mysteries. However this may be, it is evident that as soon as Christianity moved into an environment characterised by these peculiarities, it would assimilate many of them, integrating them with ideas already present.

59

First the old ideas of death and resurrection are bent in the direction of a personal immortality on one side and the dying and resurrection of Christ as an incarnated God on the other. Until then those ideas were related to the vicissitudes of the group, the community. Now that feeling has begun to be more individual, all aspects of the figure of Christ become more tangible, more human. Indeed, the whole figure of Jesus comes nearer to men and can be approached with more spontaneous emotion. The love felt in respect to this divine figure, who shares the human joy and suffering, is of a quality different from the love in respect to the father-figure of the Old Testament that is to be aligned with the god-figures of the pagan world. Both those lines can perhaps be related to each other so that the father-figure arises from beliefs where the divinity is represented as totally transcendent – the Father, however loving he may be, remains always the same as for the earlier generation, a figure looked at with holy diffidence. Meanwhile the Saviour, the figure of the god who dies and resurrects, is more in line with the idea of an immanent deity, the accent falling on the mystical unity between God and man. In the latter case, faith assumes a more intimate character, signifies a more personal tie.

Piety in the Mysteries

This development confirms the arrival in a different climate, another emotional atmosphere. Reitzenstein (op.ct. p.22) describing this change, expresses it very emphatically. Concerning the piety of the mystery cults, he says, *One cannot imagine a more close relation between God and man and a feeling not only of lifelong gratitude but even of personal love.* Furthermore he speaks about their message of salvation by God for the individual human being; about collections of sacred books which were used in the rituals; about faith in the venerated deity as a personal act of trust and surrender, inspired by experiences in the mystery drama. He also speaks about thanksgivings; preaching as exegesis of holy texts; about mission; about a standard form of confession, which ties the community together; about the miracle tales which were passed round and finally about the accounts of personal visions.

Thus, in those mystery communities, there is already an intimacy inspired by salvation bestowed in previous distress. There is talk of grace, received undeserved and of a love which has not first to be proven, but which one receives from the deity. Only afterwards - out of a feeling of gratitude - the love for one's fellow man begins to flourish. No doubt this affection also coloured the figure of Christ. The fact that slaves and women could take part in the mystery communities was also influential. Indeed, where other deities often bear a very pronounced masculine character, in Christianity the figure of Jesus shows feminine as well as masculine traits, which can surely be attributed to the composition of the community. It is quite natural that the slaves, who became members, began to see the figure of the Lord as liberator and surely also as the co-sufferer in their distress. All this resonates in the descriptions in the Gospels when the figure of the Saviour takes form. Everyone, even the least community member, has, so to speak, co-operated therein. It has been the poetical imagination of the community that, by the interaction of all the emotional factors described in the preceding chapters, shaped the figure of Christ into what he has become for us.

Orpheus-like figures are also used, mixed with figures from the Old Testament.

Christ as ideal figure

Little by little the pattern begins to become clear. Christ was becoming more and more the ideal figure, onto whom all longings and needs of the community that venerated him are transferred and on whom the fulfilment of these longings is projected. The termination of religious longing is always communion, a becoming one with the deity, who, it was assumed, appeared in Christ.

The final stage of religious development

It was mentioned above that this communion could be so close and intimate that it was compared with the bond of marriage. In the ecstasy of this bonding, where the ego-consciousness is switched off, there can be total merging in the being of the venerated deity. The final stage is that God and man for human consciousness become one. Indeed, considered in its pure state, this mystical union is the crown upon the whole religious life. Mark well, considered in its pure state. That is to say, this becoming one inwardly is pure only if it reveals itself outwardly as the relation between a living God (as spirit of Christ) and an energetic man. Here and there this is indeed achieved. Namely where the true knowledge of God and his secrets is not an occult thing, but the eternal activity of the infinite spirit that reveals itself in the finite human spirit. The beholding of the deity and the truth becomes transformed in this living unification. Then many words are silenced which one had devoted, mostly immaturely, to this unification. This is the final religious development, where a person following the road of symbolism, learns to consider the symbols as superfluous.

The symbol of Christ becomes superfluous too, on this ultimate level.

CHAPTER IX

Epilogue

The birth of the Church

Rejection of the Christians by the Jewish Synagogue

W. Föster (1955) in his article, "The essence of Gnosticism", says that sometimes, by means of the allegorical method, one culture could adapt material taken from other cultures for it's own purposes. Certainly this was the case with Christianity, which took over the Jewish holy scriptures but expounded them in an anti-Jewish spirit, turning them against the Jews. Although this was done partly by liberal Jews themselves, as we have seen, it remained nevertheless extremely serious for orthodox Jews. So it was quite comprehensible that Judaism began to defend itself vigorously. Particularly because the attack on the orthodox came not only from those we might call Christians, but at the same time from the numerous gnostic sects which, even for their contemporaries, were not easily distinguishable one from another. Their most important aspect was that they all corrupted the letter of the law and therefore made it powerless.

When confusion became evident because of the multitude of sects, on the Jewish side measures had to be taken. For the whole of Judaism risked becoming merged into one world religion, out of which all national elements would have been dispelled. In the eyes of the conservatives these elements would have been replaced by nothing of real value.

The definition of a Jewish canon

First, rejection of the very extensive literature, compiled step by step in the Greek language and spirit, had to be achieved.

Much of this was considered by the adherents as holy scriptures, because many were assumed to be literally inspired by the Lord of the community, Jesus. Others were attributed to other persons of authority. Clearly, limits had to be drawn or, as it was put, 'a wall built around the Law'. This happened, about 90 CE. at the synod of Jamnia (Jabne). The Jews of that time were familiar with two collections of holy texts:- first 'the Law' – the five books of Moses - and secondly the writings of the prophets. Now, step by step, there appeared a considerable number of texts which were considered as *inspired*, but were never put together as a closed collection. This last group, called 'the scriptures', was still open and everything that claimed to have authority, or was considered by the community as such, was included. Gradually this collection became too extensive and the orthodox felt themselves, quite understandably, threatened by the ongoing symbolising promoted in those texts. What should be the determining factor for inclusion? The criterion for this was found in the so-called prophetic succession, i.e. the succession of the respective prophets, who passed their inspiration on to the next one, with or without the 'laying on of hands'. Even when this succession was not fully known, it was considered to have begun with Moses and ended with Ezra. There the inspiration stopped and also 'the scriptures'. What was written later – or was supposed to have been written later – could not be recognized as inspired. These non-recognized scriptures contained all that might be called Christian literature; not only all sorts of revelations which we do not find in the New Testament, but also other Gospels, even when they were not mentioned as such. From that point on there existed a clearly defined Jewish canon, and what was written in the collection of these books became the criterion for the assessing other non-canonical books. The leading idea was, that the authors of the canonic literature had not written a single letter voluntarily, but had served selflessly as instruments of God's spirit when writing. By this criterion a quite extensive literature was condemned.

A cursing formula against Christians

Even this did not seem to be sufficient. The president of the synod at Jamnia proposed the insertion of a cursing formula in the so-called 'Sjemone-Esree', the daily prayer composed of eighteen passages. The following phrase came spontaneously from those attending: 'May the heretics have no hope' (see Berachôt 4:3, also Friedländer Gnosticismus, p.93). This meant the banishing, in the strictest sense of the word, of Christians from the Jewish community. As a consequence of this it was forbidden to trade with the Minim and, in the case of illness to be treated, healed or cured by them (see Friedländer, op.cit. p.95). Thus, the infant Christianity now stood, newborn, alone in the world, while the 'mother' who gave birth to it, had disowned it. Therefore Jesus, representing Christianity, could say to his mother (John 2:4) *That is your concern, Mother, not mine* (even stronger in the Dutch translation: *Woman, what have I to do with you!*). This separation occurred about 100CE and, once more, the scene changed.

The Roman Catholic Church in statu nascendi

Rome as centre

Earlier it had been the Jews who played the leading role in the development of ideas; then that role was taken over by the proselytes stemming from a Greek cultural background, making the Greek element dominant; finally the Roman element made its entrance. There had been, since Alexandria became part of the Roman empire, a strong rivalry between this city and the capital. The leading role in spiritual development moved gradually from the oriental city to the metropolis - Rome. There all the peoples and tribes of the known world swirled around and mixed, even more than in Alexandria. This happened, not intentionally but naturally, as is usually the case in history.

The communities of the New Covenant, which by now were being called Christian, stood alone. They had always considered themselves and their teaching against the background of Judaism, from which they differentiated themselves. Their originality consisted for a large part in denying the old received laws and prohibitions. The organization that had supported them fell away; a new organization was still lacking. Reflection on their own religious tradition began and also, on a small scale, gatherings were held with sympathizers, in the manner of the mystery communities. Provincial synods were held; some organization of the communities was also put in place, where it had not been taken over from the Jewish synagogue. This must have been a rather long period. Since the organization followed that of the Roman Empire – i.e. by provinces – it finally arrived quite naturally at Rome as the city the most appropriate to take the lead.

The sound doctrine: Rejection of gnosticism

Meanwhile many things could and did happen. A reflection of this can be found in the latest written parts of the New Testament, the pastoral letters (1 and 2 Timothy and Titus). In those there is no longer a question of Jewish influence, Christianity was long since free from it. The Pauline direction had prevailed on the whole front, more specifically of course, since the Jewish influence was no longer asserted – as Judaism having cut off the upstart religious movement. There were still deacons, apostles and teachers, functions which were also known in the Jewish communities. Beside this a new hierarchy of functions was created, which could be characterized as Roman: Bishops ('epi-scopi' = over-seers), one of whom will later become the principal bishop, and, subject to him, a whole hierarchy of offices was installed, of which the rights and duties were strictly defined. Here the Roman mentality became dominant, as also happened concerning doctrine and daily life. As for this last aspect, the idea of the end of time – eschatology, the end of this world, a concept of Jewish origin - receded into the background. The pragmatic pastoral leaders of the community were now teaching their 'flock' to live in the present, and to find there their task and happiness. This was called the *wholesome doctrine* that had to be preached (Titus 2:1). Both Titus and Timothy were educated as future bishops following this teaching. This *wholesome doctrine* contained more. It was also applied to all spiritualization, which was to be abolished once and for all. In order to know where one stood, reality was moved into the foreground. If there was to be talk of a great man of the past, Jesus called the Christ, the Saviour and leader of the faithful, then this must be a real person, not a vague great figure out of an obscure past.

Transmuting Jesus into an historic figure

This raised questions concerning the time when Jesus, about whom the faith preached so much, lived and worked. There were two fixed points. Jesus must have lived after John the Baptist, who

66

had announced Jesus' coming and John's communities of disciples were in several ways e.g. by their baptism, preparing for the Christians. John had been killed, according to the historian Josephus, in the year 30. The mission of Jesus must have taken place thereafter. This must have happen before the year 70, because everything could be seen to indicate that the fall of Jerusalem was punishment for having killed the Messiah. Thus, the year following the activities of John emerged, the year known as the *year of the Lord's favour* (Is. 61:2). In addition, Jesus acted in continuation of the work of John. Here the Roman calendar was to play its role as it was known that Jesus was crucified under Pontius Pilate: so he must have been born a human age earlier, say thirty years, in the year Quirinius was governor. In any case this story had to be made as real as possible, the life and works of Jesus had to make a continuous story. The dying and the resurrection, plus a couple of bundles of sayings he might have said and some symbolic deeds - which perhaps should not be taken for real - were not enough. That wouldn't give the multitude any real grip; they asked for facts, not ideas in symbolic form. The portrait must be filled in, if it was to appeal to the people.

Marcion: organization and Canon

It is at this point that Marcion[10] came in. He was a rich ship owner from Pontus who came to Rome and was for some time a member and even a leading person in the community there. He organized the community and many others in the empire in a strict Pauline spirit. Since the Jews had rejected Christianity, Judaism should be banished as much as possible from the Christian scriptures. Away with the Old Testament, as this was composed by the synod of Jamnia, contradicting the Greek translation of the Septuagint! Away with preaching the God of war and violence! Who would want to keep all this, obscuring their own Christian teaching? Only one gospel was composed, naturally out of the elements which were, as we saw, available. It was the heart of the gospel which we call Luke, which of all the gospels we know, was the most favourable towards the pagans and the least oriented towards Judaism. In addition to this one gospel, a number of letters from Paul were also accepted for this new Christian canon. On this basis

Marcion, in great style, presented the first organization of the texts to the new communities.

Taking over elements from other religious groups

Nevertheless this organization was, in the eyes of the rising Roman church, not strong enough, especially in order to resist the rivalry of other flourishing religious cults such as Mithraism. Elements of the mystery cults were imperceptibly integrated into the young Christianity, for example the Lord's supper. Thus a variety of elements from different sources were together drawn into Christianity. The statement of the early ecclesiastical writer Lactantious, seems to be true: 'What was found sporadically about truth before Christ had been elaborated in Christianity to become one integrated whole'. This happened under and through the Roman organizing spirit and in this way the Roman Catholic Church took shape. This 'general' church, could embrace all ideas alive in the whole empire, in a certain form, but could firmly reject them in any other form.

The three pillars

Risk of persecution

There was, however, yet another specific reason why it was time to arrive at a rigorous ordering of the new faith. This was the dangerous risk of persecution by the Roman state. The fact was that the Jewish religion, in spite of the submission of the Jewish nation, was still an accepted, tolerated, religion. As long as Christianity saw itself as a radical trend within the Jewish community, and was also considered as such by the outside world, the Christian communities could live under the cloak of Judaism. But when Christianity had been banished from Judaism and had to stand alone, it was confronted face to face with the Roman state. This was occurring in cases where Christians were accused, for instance, of refusing to adore the emperor as a god. The Roman authorities, not being satisfied with a more or less mystical explanation of faith, not always identical in the different communities, required a clear unambiguous confession, everywhere identical. The Roman authorities demanded that the leaders of the communities bind their members strictly to this Confession, once known. This was another - external – cause of that severe and detailed organization by which the Roman church is characterized. Furthermore, the danger to which the members were exposed led to the desire that their leaders, the bishops, should act and speak in their name. Consequently the Church acquired an authoritarian relationship between governors and governed, more or less a copy of the existing state. This process continued until, under Constantine the Great, church and state become one.

First pillar: A Christian canon

Among subjects of common interest which the bishops had to settle during their regular meetings was the relation to the Old Testament, which had been cut off by Marcion. This excision was found to be a disadvantage to the new religion, precisely because it was the Old Testament which described the beginning of the world and made a great impression on all sorts of pagan peoples. Christians had learned to understand the symbolic and this was the very reason the rabbinate had confined itself to the literal meaning of the collection of sacred scriptures and to the Hebrew text, fixed and agreed for all time. The Old Testament had been rejected by Marcion, who saw that, taken literally, it had too many offensive passages. The Christian leaders therefore decided to rehabilitate the Old Testament, but with a symbolic exegesis. That is, using the allegorical method and placing it next to their own Christian canon. which they took over from Marcion. They enlarged this with letters and gospels which had a less outspoken anti-Jewish character. Some books were for a long time the subject of controversy. Leaving aside the peculiarities concerning these debates I simply note here that through them the existing Christian Bible, Old and New Testaments, were established.

Second pillar: authority of the bishop

From these beginnings the bishops progressively became the absolute and unchallenged rulers of the community, because in the hour of danger the vigorous leadership of those energetic men was needed. In the course of time the bishops, especially when they met, assumed an authority based on the doctrine of the Apostolic succession. This postulates that, beginning with Peter, the putative first bishop of Rome, a successor always holds his chair and each one passes on his divine authority to his successor. The office of bishop became, in this way, sacred and unassailable.

A consequence of this was also that, in front of a judge, one could name the founder of the new religion. For, according to the Gospel(Mat.16:13-20), Peter was appointed by Christ himself to lead the church. This well known passage must have been inserted into the gospel at this time. So Christ was now also seen as the founder of the church and the demand, not only of the judge, but also of the multitude of community members could thus be answered. This multitude could otherwise not imagine the establishment of the community. Once this was accepted, the idea that the divine Logos had been incarnated respectively in several people (the prophets) and groups (e.g. the Christian community itself) was abandoned. Instead the thesis emerged that this was exceptionally the case with the person of Jesus; taken even to the greater extreme, that God himself, in all his fullness, was incarnate in Jesus.

Third pillar: The symbolum

Only one thing was still needed to achieve the building of the Roman church: a *symbolum*[11] - that is, a short formulation of belief by which the faithful could be bound, so that the same belief could be professed everywhere. Two of the pillars upon which the Roman Church rested were already present:- the episcopal dignity – *where the bishop is, there is the church* - and the Canon as a well-defined body of literature, against which new ideas and scriptures could be tested. The third pillar was still lacking:- the Articles of Faith, which summarized the confessed truth, briefly and indubitably. The result – leaving out the details of the process – is the Confession of the Apostles, the third pillar on which the Church today still rests.

This 'regula fidei' presented 'facts', in contrast to the earlier church's mystical ideas lacking a factual base. This rule of belief was vigorously directed against the spirit of the previous period, characterized by searching for the hidden meaning of symbols which spoke of the divine truth in a veiled way. The multitude now got it's Gospel story that served to edify them without any idea of the deeper underlying sense. The Church had to be the Church of the many; these were not the few 'pneumatics', the 'spirituals' who understood the deeper truth by means of their higher knowledge, but the 'common' man, who felt something of the truth, but was not capable of making it sufficiently conscious so that he could make use of it in his life and act.

Résumé

Looking over the whole development, we can say that the Gospel is the affective representation in which an eternal true reason speaks. So the whole merges into symbolism. Hence, this Gospel was not suitable for the multitude, who had no *'ears to hear'* (Bolland 1897).

Drews (op.cit. pp. 377-382) says it in the following way: "The premise of Christianity is not a personality, but an idea, namely the idea of the loving God. The whole history of the Gospel has only one purpose, to open the hearts and minds of people to the idea of love" . . ."The essence of Christianity was that it brought together, into one focus, the religious ideas which were floating around in Judaism since the banishment; it took away the relative uncertainty of those ideas, introducing a credo that seemed unshakably founded upon the putative historical image of Christ" . . ."The Canon had as its purpose to secure the historical authenticity of the salvation principle as presented by the synoptists, against the gnostic spiritualization into a metaphysical abstraction".

Conclusion

So the Church slid back into the same dependency on the letter of the scriptures, against which the Gnosis was originally directed.

Notes

1. (p.4) Sennacherib, king of Assyria from 704 to 681 BCE. Sennacherib is perhaps most known by his third military campaign to Syria-Palestine in 681 BC He took several rebel cities. He besieged Jerusalem. But this city was spared on payment of a heavy tribute (See also the Bible, Kings 20: 12-18; Kings 18: 13-19; Isa.36: 1-37, 37). Sennecherib's most enduring work was the rebuilding of Niniveh and its monumental palace.

2. (p..8) Baruch about 600 BC The '*Book or Prophecy of Baruch*', is a deuteron-canonical or apocryphal text. It is not included in the Hebrew Bible, though it appears in the Septuagint and is thus an integral part of the Old Testament of Roman Catholics. Baruch wrote the book five years after the destruction of Jerusalem by Babylonia in 586.BCE. He also noted the prophesies of Jeremiah (Jer.32:12-16, 36:4-32,43:1-7 and 45).

3. (p.11) Posidonius or Poseidonius, 135-551 BCE, Greek stoic philosopher, considered the most learned man of his time, because of his encyclopedic knowledge.

4. (p.19) *Psalms of Solomon*: pseudepigraphical work, comprising 18 songs: Hymns: Thanksgiving, lamentation, admonitions and instruction, suggesting that they were used in Jewish cultic rites Belief in resurrection and free will. Associated with the conquest of Jerusalem by Pompei. The original hebrew version got los, but Greek and Syrian versions have been preserved.

5. (p.23) Galilea is the hebrew word for region.. So the correct translation of this text would be*: So he shall bring in the future honour over the road to the sea, the other side of the river Jordan,the regions of the nations* the explicit reference to Galilee as the Palestine district is absent here.. This is the 1979 version in the Dutch translation under the auspices of the Netherlands Bible Association. But already in the Septuagint we find this explicit reference to Galilee. (A mistake?) The same is the case with the Dutch translation of 1618/1619 by the National Synode at Dordrecht and with both English translations I consulted: The Holy Bible of 1611, the revised standard version of

72

1952 and The Revised English Bible of 1989, Oxford University Press.

6. (p.34) Origen (Alexandria ca. 185-Tyrus 254CE): Early Christian theologian and one of the most creative thinkers of his time. In 202 became principle of the School for Cathechism in Alexandria. Devoted his life to the formulation of the Christian faith, but in later centuries many of his points were rejected.

7. (p.34) Eusebius: from Caesarea (ca. 265-339) Bishop of Caesarea. The father of church history. His *Historia Ecclesia*, the first fundamental history of the church, is not always reliable.

8. (p.49) Minim: There is no consensus among the scientists not a consensus concerning the term Minim. There is a school among which disagrees with Friedlaender, among them Herford, the author of a book about "Christianity in Talmud and Midrasch" (London 1904). They are of the opinion that with "Minim" surely means the Jewish Christians. Friedländer contests this at several places and says that this term refers to pre-Christian Jewish gnostics. In the present author's opinion this controversy is of little importance. On the one hand Friedländer asserts that the Jewish gnosticism becomes quite naturally and unnoticed Christianity. So I do not see why he insists in making such an emphatic difference between his Jewish gnostic and the early Christians. On the other hand very little is known about the Jewish-Christians. Most of the information comes from Acts of the Apostles and the here found information is on the whole a rather legendary. It is not so inviting for a historian to make use of it. What is known is that after 125 CE, when the Barkochba mouvement was repressed, the Jewish Christians withdrew to the eastern regions of the Roman Empire Among them gnostic movements asserted themselves. In the present author's opinion the term "Minim" referred precisely to that Jewish gnosticism which led to the birth of the movement only later called Christianity. In which case both the above parties would in fact agree: The Minim were vigorously fought first by Jews and in a later periods by Christians. This was the case with gnosticism in general.

9. (p.51) Flavius Josephus (see Drews 1924 p.289) calls the devastation of Jerusalem a punishment fort the conviction of James. Though this text is clearly an interpolation, nevertheless it expresses what was in the mind of those who put it in...

10. (p.64). Marcion (85-ca.160 CE), son of the bishop of Sinope; became a prosperous ship owner. Moving about 140 to Rome, he joined the Christian community there, but repudiated it in 144 and was excommunicated as a quasi gnostic heretic. He founded his own church. The Marcionite sect became in the 2nd to the 5th century wide spread throughout Europe, Asia, Africa.. It continued to flourish until as

late as the 10th century, especially in Syrian culture. Marcion is perhaps best known for his treatment of Scripture. He rejected as hopelessly impossible. ll attempts to harmonize Jewish biblical traditions with those of Christians. He rejected the Old Testament; accepted as authentic all of the Pauline Letters and the Gospel According to Luke (after he had expurgated them of Judaic elements). His treatment of Christian literature was significant, for it forced the early church to fix an approved canon of theologically acceptable texts out of the mass of available unorganized material (After the *Encyclopeia Britannica 1974*).

11. *(p.66) Symbolum.* This Greek word was also used in the mystery services for the sacred formula which as a secret was passed on from the one to the other.

Bibliography

Bertholet, A.: *Die jüdische Religion von der Zeit Esras bis zum Zeitalter Christi,* In: *Biblische Theologie des Alten Testaments, pp. 411-414.* [The Jewish religion in the era of Esra till the era of Christ. In: Biblical Theology of the Old Testament, pp. 411-414].

Bolland, G.J.PJ. *De grote vraag aan de Christenheid van onze dagen* [The important question for the Christianity of our days].

Bonhoffer, A.: *Epiktet und das Neue Testament,* [Epicteus and the New Testament] Giessen, 1911.

Bousset, W.: *Die Bedeutung der Person Jesu für den Glauben.* [The meaning of the person of Jesus for the faith] Berlin, 1910.

Bultmann, R.: *Das Urchristliche im Rahmen der Antiken Religionen,* [The Christian essence in the frame of the antique religions] Zürich 1949.

Bergh van Eysinga, G.A. van den: *see* Van den Bergh.

Drews, A.: *Die Entstehung des Christentums aus dem Gnosticicmus,* [The birth of Christianity out of the gnosis, p.158] Jena, 1924.

Epictetus: *Zedekundig Handboekje, met fragmenten,* [Moral pocket-book with fragments; p 146; 159, 239]'s Gravenhage, 1919.

Flavius Josephus*: Bellum Judaicum II; 8, 10.*

Föster, W.: *"Das Wesen der Gnosis"* In: *Die Welt als Geschichte* ["The essence of gnosticism", in: The world as history] 1955.f

Friedlander, M.: *Zur Entstehungsgeschichte des Christentums,* [Christianity, the history of its origin; p.2; p.4]; Vienna 1894.

Friedlander, M.: *Der vorchristliche Gnosticismus,* Gottingen, 1898 [The pre-christian Gnostic].

Friedländer, M. *Geschichte der jüdischen Apologetik,* pp. 231-250.and 248-262 [History of the Jewish apologetics] Zürich 1903.

Henneke, E. *Neutestamentische Apokryphen*, *p. 437*. Tübingen, 1924.

Herford *Christianity in Talmud and Midrasch*, London, 1904.

Jonas, H.: *Gnosis und Spätantiker Geist I*, Göttingen 1954 ["Gnosis and the spirit of the late Antiquity". In here especially the chapter about "the attitude of the Gnosis towards life"].

Jonge, M.de: *H.J.Schoepf'v isie op Paulus* In: *Theologie en Practijk* Ed. " De Tijdstroom", Lochum 1959. [The vision on Paul of H.J. Schoepf].

Justinus Martyr: *Dialogus cum Tryphone*.

Kossen, H.B. *Op zoek naar de historische Jezus*, Assen, 1960 [Looking for the historical Jesus].

Leisegang: *Die Gnosis, p. 2;* 1955.

Moore, G.F.: *Judaism*, 1927/1930.

Müller, J.G.: *Die messianischen Erwartungen des Juden Philo*, Basel 1870 [The messianic expectancies of the Jew, Philo].

Pfeiderer, O: *Vorbereitung des Christentums in der Griechischen Philosophie* [Preparation for Christianity in the Greek Philosophy] Tübingen, 1906.

Pierson, Allard: *De Bergrede en andere Synoptische fragmenten*, [The sermon on the mount and other synoptic fragments] Amsterdam 18.

Proost, K.F.: *De betekenis van Jezus Christus voor ons geloofsleven*, [The meaning of Jesus Christ for our religious life] Zeist 1919.

Proost, K.F.: *Tussen twee werelden – Philo Judaeus;* Arnhem 1952. [Between two worlds – Philo Judaeus].

Promus: *De Entstehung des Christentums*, 1905 [The origin of Christianity].

Quispel, G.:*Gnosis als Weltreligion*, [Gnosis as world religion; p.21] Zürich, 1951.

Raschke, H.: *Das Christusmysterium*, [The Christ mysrtery] Bremen, 1954 [The Christ mystery] Bremen 1954..

Reitzenstein, R.: *Die Hellenistischen Mysterienreligionen*, [The hellenistic mystery-religions; p16; p.17; p.240]; Leipzig, 1927.

Schoeps, H.J. *Urgemeinde, Judenchristentum, Gnosis*, Tubingen, 1956. [Primaeval community, Jewish Christianity, Gnosis].

Schürer: *Geschichte des jüdischen Volkes im Zeitalter Jesu Christi II; pp. 601-603 and pp. 648-671* [History of the Jewish people in the period of Jesus Christ].

Schweitzer, A. *Geschichte der Leben Jesu Forschung*, Tubingen, 1911 [Research history about the life of Jesus] p. 56; p.525 & 641.

Schweitzer, A.:*Die Mystik des Apostels Paulus* [The mystic of Paul], 1930.

Seneca, L. Annaeus: *Opera; Volumen Secundum (*continet libros: **De Beneficiis, De Clementia, De Ira)**. Annotated edition by Carolus Rudolphus Fickert (in Latin(Lipsiae, MDCCCXLIII (Leipzig, 1843).

Troeltsch, E.:*Die Bedeutung der Geschichtlichkeit Jesu fur den Glauben.* [The importance of the historical existence of Jesus for the faith; p.29; p.32] Tübingen, 1911.

Van den Bergh van Eysinga, G.A.: *Voorchristelijk Christendom*, Zeist, 1918 [Pre-christian Christianity].

Van den Bergh van Eysinga, G.A.: *Leeft Jesus of heeft hij alleen maar geleefd?* 1930. [Does Jesus live or has he only lived?] Arnhem, 1930.

Van den Bergh van Eysinga, G.A.: *Het karakter der Evangeliegeschiedenis,* [The character of the gospel history] Assen, 1939.

Van der Wissel, F: *Heeft het evangelie een verborgen betekenis?* [Does the gospel have a secret meaning?] In: *Mens en Kosmos*, July 1959.

Van der Woude, A S.: *Die messianische Vorstellungen der Gemeinde von Qunram.* [Messianic expectancies of the community of Qumran] Assen, 197.

Van Wijk, A.W. *Christusbeschouwingen onder modernen,* [Modern reflections about Christ] p.124 and 125.

Wilson, R.M.L.: *The gnostic problem*, London, 1958, p.3; p.69; p.224.

Windisch, H.: *De tegenwoordige stand van het Christusprobleem*, Assen 1925 [The actual state of the Christ problem].

Summaries

IN THIS WORK THE author, in an original approach, offers a convincing argument that the story of Jesus is not a historically real one, but rather a religiously true one, confronting us with our true human nature. This powerful legend came into existence as the answer to and fulfillment of the religious needs of the developing communities of the new creed. (The New Covenant). It created the leading religious Archetype for the new era. What follows is a summary of each of the nine chapters.

1. The diaspora

This chapter describes the dispersion of the Jewish people throughout the Hellenistic cultural area. Under Roman law, Jews had a privileged position: Liberty to practise their own religious culture; freedom from adoration of the Emperor; permission to follow their own jurisprudence (excepting capital punishment).

The Jewish communities were mainly found in Greek and Egyptian cities with Alexandria as the main focus of Jewish religion. Here an intensive exchange took place between the Jewish and the Greek conceptual world with an impressive image of God, their prophets of impressive statures and a keen interest in justice, the Jews entered the tiltyard of religious syncretism.

2. Syncretism

Confrontation between representatives of different beliefs stimulated self-criticism and increased depth of belief. A sort of philosophy of religion with several different approaches developed: some holding that the human soul was just part of the divine; others stressing the transcendence of God; yet others held the dualistic view that the soul, though being a spark of the divine fire, was imprisoned int he hostile element of matter and had to be liberated from it.

Many Jewish religious representations and practices lost their credibility, e.g. the anthropomorphic image of God; the strange sacrificial ceremonies; the purely nationalistic image of the expected Messiah. Many of them lost their faith preferring an allegorical interpretation of the ancient books. The Jewish religion became one among many mystery religions. The works of the Jewish philosopher, Philo, made an important contribution to the process and our later understanding of it.

The anthropomorphic intercessions of God were attributed to the Logos, which acts and speaks for God. The Messiah developed into the image of the ideal wise man.

3. Idealization by allegorical explication

Hellenic Jews believed that the Holy Ghost always spoke in parrables. However, conservative Jews lead by the Palestine Rabbinate, repudiated this tendency. There was even a demand that those who abandoned the Law, should be banned from the Jewish community.

Stressing the importance of a moral way of living is also found in the views of non-Christian philosophers of the time such as Seneca. His: "Forgive them: all are unwise" chimes with Jewish views expressed in works like the apocryphal Psalms of Solomon: "The offer to the Lord is justice and pureness of heart and lipps" (Psalms of Solomon, 11:2). This striving for an ethical way of living finds its highest expression with the Essenes in their ideal of sobriety and community of possession.

4. The material and its elaborators

The evangelical Jesus seems to be an assemblage of passages from the Old Testament used as the building blocks. How and by whom the story of the evangelical Jesus was composed? These were communities, especially the Essenes. In these communities the expectation of the coming Kingdom of God was vividly alive. Here, one was assidiously looking for any text that might indicate the coming of the Messiah. Surprisingly, the Passion texts are not yet applied to the Messiah. However, it is evident that the evangelical Messiah figure is the result of a process of continuous reflection on prophetic prediction.

The life and acts of Jesus progress in such a way that these prophecies are indeed fulfilled. How should we react to this correlation between prophecy and the evangelical Jesus? The most plausible explanation is that the evangelical history is a legend, without a historical foundation. The figure of Jesus is not a historically real, but rather a religiously true one, being the ideal that shows us our true human nature.

5. Messiah Images

We know of several Messiah images. Philo, exponent of the Alexandrian diaspora, does not acknowledge future redemption, only a mystical, present one. He acknowledges a mediator, but this is a celestial figure, who mediates with God for the reconciliation for our sins. This figure is called the Logos. According to Philo, the Logos had incarnated himself in, for example, Joshua (=Jesus), the successor of Moses. This Johsua is the prototype of the Messiah, who will appear and be called Joshua or Jesus.. In the Epistle to the Hebrews, the Christ appears in Heaven as the true high priest. More earthly traits are absent.

The Gospel according to John speaks also of the Logos, but here as the incarnated Word. The Messiah image in Revelation, a rider robed in a garment dyed in blood with a sharp sword coming out of his mouth, breathes a Jewish spirit.

The Pauline figure of Christ is composed out of a future image of the judging Messiah coupled wth a past image of the Lord who, by his sacrifice, reconciled the faithful wth God. The question now becomes how did the evangelical Jesus become the dominant Messiah image.

6. The suffering Messiah

What is the origin of the Messiah ideal as the "man of sorrows"? In 70 A.D. the temple in Jerusalem was destroyed.. It marked the end of the national existence of the Jewish people. This traumatic event must have deeply influenced the Messiah Image. Before this event there is no question of a Christian literature with a suffering and crucified Jesus.

Palestinian Jewry is also drawn into the turmoil of syncretism: Logos wisdom and Messiah representation, both, Greek and Jewish, go through a melting process. A new type of religion is born. Here, we find the origin of Christianity.

80

The devastation of the temple was considered as a punishment of the Jewish people for their haughtiness, pretending to be the chosen people. The national Messiah fell from his pedestal. The belief in a suffering Logos developed.. God had to suffer as soon as he appears in human form in this world. Affiliations were looked for with Job and the Prophets. So the new Messiah image had to show a martyr character. In this way, the suffering community constructs out of their proper needs, its Messiah image.

7. The Lord who rises with his parish

The believers who read the Old Testament as a continuous allegory developed into the community of the New Covenant. When speaking here of "Resurrection", it is not only an event,, but also the metamorphosis out of a sinful into a God-worthy life. Resurrection concerns the Spirit, who as the spirit of truth, always has to suffer and suffers in its community, symbolically spoken of as "in its body", i.e., the community as the temple of God. This community – being the body of Christ -- rises togetheer with the Lord. The resurrection happens as soon as the members consider themselves as the new community. This comes about, if separated from the offiicial synagogue, a number of people assemble and recognise that they are striving for something quite different from the original group. One realises that the new community of God is risen..

The Rabbinate also l recognizes this change and it is on guard against those antinomian gnostics. Reciprocal accusations follow, culminating with the Christian accusing the Jew of killing the Lord Jesus. When the rabbinate takes measures to exclude those modernists, the Christian church is born out of the communities of the new covenant.

8. The new creed

Very soon the new communities are mainly composed of pagan-Christians, often stemming from other mystery religions. What were the religious needs of this group? First a strong need for redemption: being liberated from matter, from guilt, from fate. The image of a god of mercy dominated with the theme of a dying and resurrecting God, where the initiated had to go through this suffering and dying themselves. A moral pessimism prevailed. One was thoroughly impressed by the general sinfulness of humanity. We uncover this pessimism in Paul. Death and resurrection, originally associated with the community, acquire a more individual meaning.

These mystery communities are characterized by an intimate, mystic bond between God and man. At the same time further characterized by a Grace that is given undeserved and by a Love that has not to be proved, but which one receives from the Godhead.. Out of thankfulness for these two blessings burst the love for the neighbour. Of course this affectional climate also coloured the image of Christ, The Christ becomes more and more the ideal figure, bearer of the longings of the community.. This culminates in the commune, the fusion with the Godhead, whom one knew to have appeared in Christ.

9. The birth of the church

To defend Jewish orthodoxy, the rabbinate decided to demarcate all religious literature at Ezra. All Christian literature was immediately not canonical. This exclusion forced the Christian to reflect on their religious patrimony and to organize themselves independently. They instituted a hierarchical organization with the dominant position of the Bishop modelled on the organization of the Roman Empire with Rome as the centre.

No longer being Jew, how should Christians legitimate themselves in the minds of the Roman state? Clarity about the life and message of Jesus was needed. Because data were missing, one fixed dates by extrapolating backwards from the death of John the Baptist, to the birth of Jesus in the year that Quirinius was Governor. At the same time Marcion wrote the (first?) life history of Jesus. The figure of Jesus was getting filled in.. Though Marcion rejected the Scriptures of the Old Testament as being too Jewish, later Councils not only accepted four gospels but also the books of the Old Testament, resulting in our Bible. The Canon and the authority of the Bishops was in place but a profession of faith was still missing. To meet this need, the so-called "Apostles' Creed" was accepted. The three pillars on which the Roman Church rests were complete. The Church should be the church for the many,, not for the small group of initiates who were able to understand the deeper truth. Ultimately, the Church slid back into the same dependency on the letter which the gnosis tried to overcome.